# without
# Tim:

A Son's Fall to Suicide,
*A Mother's Rise from Grief*

LISA SCHENKE

# Praise for Lisa Schenke
## with*out*
# Tim

This book, written from a mother's perspective, is both a tool survivors can use in their healing process and professionals can use to understand, in detail, what families and communities go through after losing someone to suicide. Lisa's loss is palpable as she shares the decisions, feelings, and life adjustments that accompany losing her son. She takes the reader through the broad spectrum of emotions one experiences during the process of grieving and healing. This memoir acknowledges the complex nature of suicide and is written in a straightforward and responsible manner.

*—Erin MacInnes,*
*Former Director of Florida's Statewide Office of Suicide Prevention,*
*Executive Office of the Governor*

"Not since Iris Bolton's *My Son, My Son* has a book about the suicide of a child seemed sincerely authentic, warts and all. I am thankful to Michelle Linn-Gust, American Association of Suicidology President, for sending Lisa my way. I was recently sent a published book to review for AAS, and it was such a struggle. The author tried too hard or something, unlike Lisa's sincere voice in *Without Tim*. While reading, I immediately felt close to Lisa, though we couldn't be more different in our immediate responses to stress! Lisa's book reads like a movie... I can picture her house, her dogs, etc., but there's not a lot of description. I just have a feel. That's rare."

*—Ginny Sparrow,*
*Editor, American Association of Suicidology*

In this unflinchingly honest and compassionate memoir, Lisa Schenke bravely tells the story of her teenage son's suicide and a community rocked by a "suicide epidemic." This is a story I would give to other survivors, knowing they would find comfort in this unvarnished appraisal of families who struggle, love, and are unable to control the lives of those they love. This book is for parents, teens, educators, clergy, and counselors who seek to understand the tragic loss of young lives. A tribute to her son breathes in every syllable as she teaches us that a network of family, faith, and community can support us through loss and help us reach one another in our darkest moments.

—*Nancy Devor, M.Div., Ph.D.,*
*Vice President, The Samaritan Institute (a national ministry of behavioral healthcare), Former faculty member and executive director, The Danielsen Institute at Boston University*

"Grief yields way to resilience, faith and belief–through simple language and truthful observations, *Without Tim* gives us honest, everyday insights into the heartbreaking and often perplexing world of teenage depression and suicide while inspiring the reader with a very personal yet relatable look at a mother's tireless fight to make sense of it all."

—*Nicole Romaine Settembrino,*
*Co-Director, 2NDFLOOR Youth Helpline*

Lisa Schenke's memoir of her son Tim, who took his life in 2008, is a deeply moving, honest, and thoughtful reflection on what is surely the greatest possible adversity life can give a parent. Her loving tribute also offers deep lessons for those affected by the suicide of a loved one. Out of the terrible ordeal, Schenke helps herself and her readers achieve not only a heightened understanding and ability to endure, but a capacity to embrace life, on the other side of tragedy, fully and courageously.

—*Jim Laughlin,*
*Director of Communications, The Life is good Company*

*To my middle child, Peter, and my youngest child, David. Embrace life, pursue happiness, and know that I will always be there for you.*

# Acknowledgments

I have so much to be grateful for! I'd like to first thank my grief counselor, friend, book advocate, and first-draft editor, David Cotton. Without you, I would not be where I am today. Thank you to my early readers, Andrea Ganguzza and Ann Scott, for such meaningful and valuable feedback. A shout-out to the Book Doctors, Arielle Eckstut and David Henry Sterry, for choosing me as the Pitchapalooza (book pitch) winner at Booktowne in Manasquan, New Jersey, in June 2011. This victory gave me the confidence and the dangling carrot to work harder than I ever thought possible to produce a high-quality product. I would also like to thank Arielle for her roles as my content editor, mentor, and overall "go-to" girl, supporting me through the entire process. I cannot count the number of hours she shared and emails we exchanged. Many thanks to my two cover designers: Emily Dayton, a friend and college student who patiently listened to me and designed the beautiful silhouettes, and Anne MacWilliams, who created the magnificent final design, which I could not be happier with. Thank you to Califia Suntree for the thorough copyedit, Margo Rowder for the superb proofreading, and 52Novels for the wonderful formatting job.

Thank you to my children, Peter and David, for not only surviving, but thriving, and for embracing life and all the beauty it has to offer. And most of all, thank you to my husband, Andy, for just being there; being the silent, supportive partner who puts up with all of my emotions, brainstorms, and soul-searching activities. Eternally, thank you to my firstborn, Tim, for remaining a loving, innermost part of me every day. I am grateful for the infrequent but significant signs, especially hearing my song, which is now our song, on the day I finalized the title of the book. Thank you Tim for providing me with the strength to take on this enormous, self-fulfilling journey, which I hope will help many others.

Peace,

Lisa

# Prologue

In science, we tend to rely on statistics to tell us how big a problem is. In the case of suicide, the statistics paint a clear picture—too many young people think about, plan, and attempt suicide. Suicide is the third leading cause of death for young people ages twelve to twenty-four in the United States. Among high school students, seventeen percent of females and eleven percent of males contemplate suicide each year, thirteen percent of females and nine percent of males make a plan for suicide, and eight percent of females and five percent of males attempt suicide.

However, to the families of victims, national statistics have little bearing on their suffering. If just one person—their loved one—completed a suicide attempt that year, the heartache is the same. Lisa Schenke's fearless and heartbreaking account of her son's death by suicide brings this point into sharp focus. As her son Tim continued to slip downward into deeper depression and lost his drive to continue living, Lisa and the rest of her family struggled to understand Tim's inner turmoil and how best to help him. This is a moving account of a family in crisis, superbly written and unflinching. Ms. Schenke follows the breadcrumbs left behind by Tim before his suicide to gain insight into what he was thinking and feeling in the months and years before his death. She gives readers the opportunity to peer into the inner workings of her family and the choices, good and bad, made by everyone along the way. This is an important book that captures the human side of suicide statistics. A rare gift.

—Dr. Aaron White

Co-Author, *What Are They Thinking?!: The Straight Facts about the Risk-Taking, Social-Networking, Still-Developing Teen Brain* (W.W. Norton, March 2013) and Program Director, Underage and College Drinking Prevention Research at the National Institute on Alcohol Abuse and Alcoholism

# Part I

# Chapter 1

*April 26, 2008: Dinnertime*

"Then don't," I said as Tim walked out the door.

We had just gotten up from dinner that Saturday night. The day had been long, but productive. I had needed to stay busy as a way to prevent myself from worrying about the previous night. Andy and I attended our seventeen-year-old middle son Pete's high school lacrosse game, shopped for mulch and a few plants, and test-drove a possible new car for me. When asked to sit down to dinner, David, our youngest son who had recently turned fourteen, said he wasn't hungry because he and his friends had eaten pizza an hour or two earlier. Peter was at a friend's house, which left only Andy, Tim—our oldest—and me at the table. Our rectangular kitchen table seats six. Tonight Tim was down at his end by himself. Blank-faced and very quiet, not unusual behavior for an eighteen-year-old who was grounded, Tim began eating our steak dinner. Steak happens to be his favorite, cooked medium-rare, and I hoped he would eat well to help balance out his system.

Breaking the silence, I asked, "Did you call Theresa, or stop by Hoffman's?"

Tim replied, "No."

I next suggested, "Why don't you go see her in person, talk to her face-to-face? I think it will help if she sees you in person."

"Yeah, maybe," Tim said, unenthusiastically.

Theresa, the manager at Hoffman's Ice Cream where Tim worked part-time, had promised to put him back on the schedule two weeks earlier, but he still hadn't been given any hours. I added, "You should get a haircut before going because we know she'll say that you need one with your hair this length." Tim kind of nodded and maybe grunted a "yeah." After finishing the steak and refusing to eat his potato and salad, he went back to his room. Andy and I put the leftovers away and decided to take a quick ride to a department store that was having a closeout sale. Andy left the kitchen and headed upstairs.

Moments later Tim walked down the stairs and informed me that he was going to the nearby convenience store. Today's punishment, a severe combination of penalties because of what had transpired the night before, had stripped Tim of his car and his cell phone.

"You know you're grounded," I responded.

"I'm going anyway and I might not be back," Tim said flatly.

We'd had these conversations before, not frequently, but often enough for me to consider it a bluff. But at this point what choice did I have? Truthfully, Tim was now eighteen years old and could leave if he chose to.

"Then don't," I said in utter frustration. Or at least that's what I think I said. My exact words still remain a blur to me.

Little did I know that would be my last conversation with my first-born child. Less than an hour later, at 6:37 PM, Tim died by suicide.

# Chapter 2

*April 26, 2008: 7:00 PM*

I was in the midst of making my first purchases for Tim's dorm room at Drexel University for the fall semester, a set of sheets and a blanket, when the phone calls began.

Pete called my cell phone maybe forty-five minutes after Tim had left for the convenience store and Andy and I had headed out shopping. When I picked up the phone, he asked, "Is Tim home?" I was confused, since that was an unusual question. The last thing my two older sons ever did was to ask me about the other. When I said that I did not know, Pete abruptly hung up. Andy then called Pete back, questioning whether anything was going on. Pete responded, "I think you should come home." When pressed for more information, Pete said, "Something to do with a train…" Somewhat baffled and moderately alarmed, we headed to the checkout counter. Why I didn't just put the items down, I will never know.

As I was paying the cashier, my cell phone rang again, and Andy answered because I was in the middle of the transaction. Officer Shafer, of the Spring Lake Heights Police Department, said Tim had been in an accident and we should get home. When Andy asked what he meant,

Officer Shafer said he could not offer any more details on the phone. Heading to the car, my stomach was in knots and I knew I had to call Officer Shafer back. I was unable to ask anything else about Tim—either because I was paralyzed by fear or because I just could not handle hearing the inevitable. I only asked if Peter and David were home and if he would stay with them. He said yes to both questions, which gave me some small level of comfort. The fifteen-minute car ride home was agonizingly long. As always, for as long as I'd been with Andy (since 1977), we fell into our usual roles. I was talking and crying and Andy was quiet and not wanting to jump to any conclusions. I was certain that Tim was dead; if he had been alive we would have been told to go to the hospital, not to our home.

When we arrived home, I tried to wait for Andy so we could walk into the house together, but he was moving ever so slowly—as if he did not want to go inside. Unable to wait another moment, I entered through the mudroom and saw Officer Shafer in the kitchen. Before he could speak, I said, "He's dead; run over by a train," and Officer Shafer nodded, confirming my statement. I did not have to ask if it was suicide. That was something I had been unable to put out of my mind throughout the past three and a half months.

The next words out of my mouth were, "He's safe now." And then, "He's been taking so many risks, doing such dangerous things, and he's safe now with God." I am not an overly religious person, but I somehow believed Tim was with God. As Andy entered the room, I turned and said, "Yes, he's dead, stepped in front of a train." Andy said nothing and sat. He continued to sit for a long time, at least an hour, with his head down between his hands.

Officer Shafer asked me whom he could call, and I gave him my sister's and my sister-in-law's phone numbers. When he asked about anyone else, I said no.

I think David was sitting in front of the TV. Pete's friends, who were there when we arrived, had disappeared, and Pete was up in his room. I just assumed that they already knew, which turned out to be correct. Still in a state of shock, I started loading the dishwasher. I thought I should clean up if people would be coming over. This behavior wasn't unusual because, when I'm stressed out, I generally become rigid and resort to doing whatever tasks need to be done.

My sister-in-law had answered Officer Shafer's call and she and her family were heading over, but that would take about forty minutes. In the hours that followed, I did give several other names and numbers to Officer Shafer. And even though he had left a message for my sister, Denise, I insisted upon continuously calling myself, both her home phone and cell phone, because I was so upset that she wasn't answering. An hour or so later, after we finally spoke, Denise began the hour and a half trip down the Garden State Parkway, as did my parents and my mother-in-law, who also live in northern New Jersey. Denise, together with my sister-in-law, Laura, and a few others had devised a plan to inform the three grandparents and bring them to our house. I remember wondering if my parents would survive this. They both had physical ailments and do not deal well with trauma. The police officers who went to pick them up from their home brought oxygen just in case.

Our friend and neighbor Jerry, a police officer who works one town away and David's best friend's dad, was among the first whom I suggested Officer Shafer call. I thought maybe he could help Andy and David because I was incapable of even attempting to do so. One of Pete's teachers, Mr. Read, showed up very early on, and I suggested he go upstairs to talk to Pete. At some point Jerry told me that many other people would like to come over; they were just waiting for me to give the go-ahead. At least a hundred people appeared at our home within the next hour or two. I really have no idea since I couldn't relate to time at that point. I remember that my neck hurt. I felt stiff all over, but I especially remember the tension in my neck. A friend forced me to take some medication for my nerves, even though I was resistant. I also remember hugging everyone and being grateful for their love and concern. The first night, David slept at Jerry's house with eight or so of his close friends. I don't know if that was the right thing to do, but I suppose I chose whatever might get David through to tomorrow.

After a few hours of sleep for me, it all started again the next day. I recall getting up very early, only to find the other women who stayed at my house, my mother, mother-in-law, and sister, already up. Officer Shafer, who had also stayed all night, told me he'd be leaving at 7:00 or

7:30 AM when his shift was over. He explained that a police car would be left in front of our house for a day or two as a sign of protection for the family. I had known Officer Shafer for several years now, but I did not know him well. I remember revealing that I had always been somewhat afraid of him, but I would no longer feel that way. I knew that I'd now feel a sense of familiarity and comfort whenever I saw him around town.

I took a shower and got ready because I knew more people would be coming, and I was somehow going to have to figure out what to do next. A feeling of dread and a stabbing pain would alternate, reminding me of the reality of Tim's death. I went back upstairs to my bedroom a few times to check on Andy, and each time he was sitting on the edge of the bed with his head in his hands, his posture very similar to what I remembered the night before. When I had asked if he was OK, he said yes. When I asked him to come downstairs, he replied, "In a few minutes." Someone coaxed him down a little later that morning, but I am not sure who or when. I know I was functioning superficially quite well—showering, dressing, and talking to others—but I was completely unable to relate to Andy, Pete, or David.

While I remember being forced to eat, I did not feel any hunger for several days. It's hard to express how important it was to me to see kids come over, and to see Tim's friends, Pete's friends, and David's friends all hanging out together. There were so many teens there caring for my boys, playing *Rock Band* upstairs and ping-pong in the basement, going out for food, going bowling, and heading to a local arcade.

The downside to all this was that some of the kids were not relating to their parents, causing the parents to feel shut out. I specifically remember giving updates on the kids to some of their parents and also encouraging the kids to understand how worried the adults were about them. I vividly remember one mom explaining how completely excluded she was feeling, another worrying because she and her son had argued so severely the night before Tim's death, and my telling yet another mom that I was concerned about her son's facial expression being so flat and unchanging. It appeared that almost every parent was not only grieving over Tim, but also worried sick about the impact his death was having on his or her child. Because I myself had two other teens as well, I was both the grieving parent *and* the parent worried about my children. I questioned whether I would have the courage, the energy, or the sanity to continue raising adolescents.

Then there were our three smooth collies, Blondie, Ory, and Gordon. These soothing creatures helped ground us a little during this difficult period. Each of us—Pete, David, Andy, and I—could rely on them to seek us out, especially in the early mornings and late evenings when things quieted down. They are such mild-mannered dogs and pretty much went with the flow as visitors came and went. People who had never met the dogs commented on their calm demeanor. The dogs would usually offer a greeting then go off and try to find a quiet place to sleep. I'm sure they knew that something was wrong, and I'm certain that Blondie, our first family dog, knew that Tim was no longer present.

Jerry, our police officer friend and neighbor, was key to filling in where I was unable to function. He was usually the first to arrive each morning. He had been on disability, recovering from a seizure and getting the proper diagnosis and medications. I've joked that the timing couldn't have been better, so he could continue to be there for us. Jerry is a soft-spoken guy who has a special presence about him. It has always appeared to me that he commands the respect of his four sons without ever having to raise his voice. Jerry and David had always gotten along well. And while David wasn't talking much, he seemed to seek comfort in being near Jerry. Looking back, I consider Jerry a spiritual bodyguard or maybe a guardian angel.

So much had to be done in those first few days. Amazingly, people seemed to begin to fill the various roles necessary to move us along. We chose a friend, Dave, to be the mortician. Nancy, one of my most organized and "take charge" friends, worked on the program for the service, and another friend coordinated dinners to be provided for us. Jackie, Pete's close friend Andrew's mom, introduced us to her favorite priest because we were not regular attendees or members of any specific church. Mary, a good friend and a very religious woman, helped with all aspects of arranging the funeral service.

The aftermath of Tim's death was not at all what I had pictured. Throughout the previous three and a half months I had lived in fear, knowing that there was a possibility of Tim ending his life. He only shared his feelings about wanting to kill himself once with me. After that one honest conversation we'd had back in January, he had said he was fine to several mental health professionals, to Andy, and to me. I had never fully believed him, and I had become so bitter, so frustrated, so angry, and so helpless during those few months that I imagined I would want to see absolutely *no one* if Tim took his own life. But here it was, just the opposite—by midnight on that first day, I had taken in so much true affection and care from what had become hundreds of people.

# Chapter 3

Memorials were being built in several places: the elementary school, the high school, and the railroad tracks. We live in a small, tight-knit community in Monmouth County, New Jersey, where almost everyone knows one another. Our elementary school, Spring Lake Heights School, only graduated forty-five to fifty-five eighth-grade students each year at the time my boys were there, and I believe it is even fewer now. The high school, Manasquan High School, is made up of students from seven small towns and graduates approximately 230 to 250 students per year. MHS, the Warriors, is steeped in tradition and well-known for sports, most notably its years of football championships.

The memorials at the schools and at the railroad tracks were made up of fresh flowers, candles, handwritten notes, T-shirts, and uniform shirts representing town and school pride. Because we still hadn't left the house, a friend brought me pictures of the high school, which showed the memorials and the chalk tributes to "Schenker" all over the outside of the building. How I wished Tim could have felt the love he had received and understood the pain he had caused. I do believe he knows now, and I wonder if he wishes he had done things differently.

Kids needed places to gather, so churches opened their doors, and the community support was outstanding. Religious leaders and local counselors seemed to be everywhere. Without either of my sons speaking to me directly about their feelings, it was hard to evaluate their mental states. Adult friends seemed to indicate that Pete was talking to a lot of people and asking for spiritual support, while David seemed to be trying to run away from all this madness. I was told that Pete spoke to a group that gathered at Spring Lake Heights School asking them to "keep your friends close but keep your family closer," admitting that he wished he had done just that. Both boys were in and out a lot those first few days. After David had slept at Jerry's for two or three nights, I had to insist that he return to his own room and his own bed. I remember David saying, "I don't want to be here." I tried to comfort him and said, "You have to try. We'll all get used to it without Tim."

Andy and I needed our own spiritual support. When we first spoke to Father Brian the day after Tim's death, I anxiously asked him if Tim could go to heaven. Having been raised as a Catholic, I knew that taking one's own life was a mortal sin. Father Brian assured me that Tim was in heaven, that God forgives, and Tim would not be denied going to heaven because he had been in such an unhealthy mental state. I probably asked that question several times throughout those first few days, and I know my mother still struggles with it today. Father Brian prayed aloud with Andy and me, and I believe those voiced prayers helped Andy to "spring back to life." From that point forward Andy seemed to begin to function again—to acknowledge what was happening, to perform simple tasks, and to interact with others. I prayed frequently, mostly at night when I was unable to sleep. I repeated three prayers: the Our Father, the Hail Mary, and the Act of Contrition. I was most familiar with them because I had learned them as a child and prayed on and off during my lifetime. I trusted God to take care of Tim, and I believe that trust helped me tremendously.

The day after we met with Father Brian, Monday, April 28, we finally left the house in order to go to the funeral home. On our way back we drove by the railroad tracks. I pass there frequently in my daily travels, and I felt I wanted to get the first crossing over with. My mode of operation tends to be "the sooner the better." I usually prefer to face difficult situations and conflicts head-on, and this occasion was no different. The flowers and sentiments there were beautiful, and the site didn't seem to shake me up any worse than I already was. Hanging on a telephone pole was a Hoffman's uniform shirt, which had written on it in black marker, "WE LOVE YOU TIM." Hoffman's Ice Cream, where Tim worked since he was fourteen, and which is only about one-fifth of a mile from where he died, is a cornerstone of our community. It is by far the most popular ice cream shop in the area. During the summer months the line extends out the door day and night. Many of the local sports teams celebrate victories at Hoffman's, and when kids are old enough to ride their bicycles across State Highway 71, a thirty-five- to forty-mile-per-hour road, it's always one of their first destinations. Seeing a Hoffman's uniform dedicated to Tim's memory seemed exactly fitting.

# Chapter 4

*April 28–May 1, 2008*

Early in the mornings, I tried to read the cards and notes that had come in the day before. I fondly remember a letter from Arianna, a friend and student who had been tutored by Tim in geometry twice per week for the entire school year. Arianna explained that Tim was both serious and fun; they had shared their love of watching sports on TV and often spent a few minutes discussing the previous night's hockey game. She stated that unless Tim was absent from school, he never missed a scheduled session. I later found out that Arianna had failed a quiz during one of his absences, and she wondered how she would complete the geometry course without him.

I remember a few other notes clearly as well. The first was from a friend, Carol, sharing loving feelings and information about her brother's suicide. Carol felt that if her brother could have given himself more time to work things out, he would have become happy again. She expressed how she felt similarly about Tim. Another note was from a fellow member of the National Honor Society, Leslie, who was a year older than Tim. Leslie explained that she watched Tim all through elementary school and high school and saw more in him than anyone in his class. She felt he was absolutely brilliant and also very funny. Ashley, a friend of Tim's who is the sister of Amber, Tim's first girlfriend, and Logan, one of Tim's closest friends, wrote a beautiful note. She expressed warmhearted memories of Tim throughout the years we lived in Spring Lake Heights, up to and including the night before he died. She and Tim had been at the same sweet sixteen party the night before Tim died and laughed and hugged as they always had. Ashley stated that she will always remember Tim being happy and having a big smile. She also commended me for helping Tim to become the best that he could be. A note from my friend Lorie explained that her religious education director rarely uses the word death. Instead, she says, "born into eternal life," and Lorie was praying for peace for Tim in his eternal life.

In addition to reading in the mornings, I also tried to record who brought each item of food, each flower, and each gift. The job of secretary was left to me; no one else seemed to fall naturally into that role, but that was OK. Organization is one of my strong suits, and I doubt I'd have ever been able to delegate that responsibility anyway. However, I did fret as I wrote thank-you notes later, worrying that I would forget to thank someone for a gift that was personal and heartfelt.

While reading the cards the third or fourth morning, I was able to resolve one of the open issues that had been grating on me. Mary was helping with all of the details for the service, and Nancy was setting up the program—two pieces of the memorial preparation that seemed to go hand-in-hand. However, I was having the hardest time choosing a song, poem, or sentiment to put on the back cover of the program. Nancy was kind enough to go through Tim's iPod, trying to find songs he liked that would be appropriate for playing inside a church. The choices were slim, and nothing was hitting the spot for me. That morning I began reading a packet of beautiful notes and poems from David's classmates. As I read a poem titled "Always Remember," which had been found on the internet by one of David's friends, Emma, I immediately knew I wanted it for the back cover of the program. The poem reads as follows:

*Always remember to forget*
the things that made you sad.
But never forget to REMEMBER

the things that made you glad…
*Always remember to forget*
the friends that proved untrue.
But don't forget to REMEMBER
those that have stuck by you…
*Always remember to forget*
the troubles that have passed away.
But never forget to REMEMBER
the blessings that come each day…
—Anonymous

Now all that was left was to write Tim's obituary, which I simply couldn't bring myself to do. Our mortician friend, Dave, basically wrote it for me. I don't know if the obstacles were more emotional or physical; probably both. The demands on me to make decisions, coupled with the number of people in and out of my house, just didn't allow me to take the time to concentrate on it. Dave asked the necessary details, put the obituary together, and submitted it to the newspapers. It was factual, but I feel it did not contain enough loving and caring thoughts. To this day, every time I read an obituary for someone we know, I wish Tim's had been more personal, more special.

The hardest, yet in some ways the happiest, part of that first week was May 1, my forty-eighth birthday. I tried to arrange the funeral service for that day, but the logistics did not work out and we had to wait until May 2. When friends asked why I'd want it on my birthday, I explained that I would always associate my birthday with the anniversary of Tim's death anyway, so why not combine the two. My only request for my birthday was to take a bike ride in the morning. After that I did not want any recognition or celebration. As Andy and I headed out on our bikes, our first stop was the memorial at the railroad tracks.

Bike riding is my passion, and I was proud of myself for having now crossed the tracks by car and by bicycle. In addition to the memorials we had already seen, the most touching poem I have ever read was placed at the site. It read:

From form, into the formless,
Now you and spirit become one,
But oh, how we grieve here on earth,
You were EVERY MOTHER'S SON…

Days later, when I was driving by, I stopped and copied down the poem. As the months passed on, Andy and I tried to take care of that poem. At one point we reframed the original sheet of paper and covered the new frame tightly with layers of plastic. Eventually we removed it after several attempts to preserve it had failed. Although we could no longer maintain the frame, I passed along the beautiful poem by emailing it to numerous friends and sharing it on Tim's Facebook memorial page.

As for my birthday, that afternoon Andy and I had promised to buy David a TV for his room. Each of my boys was allowed to request a TV for their bedroom as their eighth-grade graduation gift. David was about seven weeks shy of finishing eighth grade, but due to the circumstances we jumped right on it. While we were at the store, David began to feel extremely ill; he was cold, very white, and shaking severely. I called our pediatrician and we headed directly to the office. When we first arrived, the thermometer did not register a fever. The doctor agreed that David's body was in some type of delayed state of shock. Rather than sending him to the hospital, our doctor decided just to observe him for a little while. I was somehow able to remain calm. I am certain that I was still numb; it was well into the following week when my range of emotions began to kick in. Oddly enough, David did develop a fever of 102 degrees during a half-hour period. The doctor was comfortable with sending him home now that the fever had developed, because the shaking had subsided and his body was now trying to fight some type of virus or infection.

Almost immediately after we arrived home, a large group of teens came in with a giant-sized homemade birthday card and one of the largest bouquets of flowers I had ever seen. I will always remember that moment as the first time since Tim had died that I felt a bit of pleasure. It's hard to explain how aware I was of feeling a little bit *good* and how guilty and uneasy I felt at the same time. I would continue to have those guilty and uneasy feelings when experiencing any sense of joy throughout the next several months.

The evening of my birthday, numerous people stopped by and gave me birthday presents. I received more meaningful gifts that year than any other. It was a beautiful night, and the teens had decided to play manhunt outside. Manhunt is sort of a combination of hide-and-seek and tag played by older children. As I looked out and watched the kids, I completely lost it. Tim absolutely loved manhunt, and I just could not tolerate that he was missing this. It almost seemed unfair that his death had brought everyone together and he couldn't be here to share it. Tim was one of the largest advocates and promoters of "Heights," the nickname for Spring Lake Heights. I felt like I could almost hear him proudly yelling, "Heights!" as the crowd laughed and played. From that night forward I would continue to have highs, such as when I received the homemade card and bouquet, followed by severe lows, as when the manhunt game began.

Coincidentally, our guinea pig, Bernard, had died the same day as Tim, but earlier in the day. We had placed Bernard in a shoe box out in the yard for burial in the near future. One of the first things Andy and I remember laughing about was people asking us why there was an empty cage in the house. Not that it was actually funny, but it *was* somewhat absurd to say that our guinea pig had died but we hadn't had the time, the memory, or the energy to deal with the cage. These small feelings of lightness and laughter during those first few days were significant to me because they showed that Andy and I were capable of sharing some connected sense of humor. The sense of pleasure I had experienced when I received the large birthday card and bouquet was different because that was private, only within me. I am grateful to that little guinea pig for giving *us* this seed of hope.

# Chapter 5

*May 2, 2008*

The day after my birthday, Friday, the memorial service was scheduled for 7:00 PM. I chose an evening service because I knew so many students and teachers would want to attend. I was not in favor of having a meal, what I have always referred to as the "after party." I've never felt comfortable eating a meal and making small talk after attending a funeral. However, we did invite out-of-town friends and family back to the house for coffee. We wanted to spend a little time with those who had traveled a distance and who we had not seen during the prior six days. How could it possibly have been only six days?

The hardest part of an evening service was the waiting, especially waiting to leave our house in the limousine to drive to the church. When we had been planning for the limousine earlier in the week at the funeral home, we were told that it could hold seven people. My first response was, "We're five." Both Andy and the mortician corrected me and said, "No, we/you are four." Immediately, the persistent stomachache worsened. We later decided that the four of us and the three grandparents would ride in the limousine.

As we arrived, I was overwhelmed. I could not believe the number of people outside the church who could not fit inside. I was later told that at least twelve hundred people were in attendance. Unfortunately, we were not able to come up with a large enough setting to hold everyone. Many were left standing outside on an unseasonably cool evening. Thankfully, speakers had been set up to allow those who stood outside to hear some of the service. Other than the obituary, the only other regret I have from that first week was the size of the church. I would love for everyone to have been held together in a warm space.

I wore the dress to Tim's funeral that I had planned to wear to his high school graduation. Ironically, I had been afraid to even purchase the dress based on the challenges we had faced the previous few months. I knew I'd never wear the dress for any other occasion, and I realized it was my *only* choice for what I'd wear to the funeral.

The service was oddly comforting. The soccer team, which Tim had been an integral part of throughout his high school years, wore their uniform jerseys and sat together in the front of the church across the aisle from us. Father Brian reminded everyone that Tim is where he should be, with God, just sooner than he should have been. Eulogies were given by Pete, Jason Bryant (who was Tim's Advanced Placement U.S. history teacher as well as his *favorite* teacher), and Brendan, one of Tim's best friends during middle school. Pete's speech focused on childhood, competitive brothers, and "Heights Pride." Jason talked about how he was immediately drawn to Tim's smile. He went on to explain that Tim was a reluctant scholar but that he and the students in Tim's classes had a glimpse of what Tim would have been like as an adult had he survived adolescence. Brendan spoke about Tim's leadership and the middle-school years, which I feel were the happiest of Tim's life. My immediate family, the grandparents, and I seemed to hold it together during the service. We cried, but somehow managed to remain composed and listen to the beautiful tribute. One of the hardest moments was watching Tim's friend Kevin burst into loud tears as they placed the urn into the limo at the end of the service. Andy, Pete, David, and I chose to greet people outside after the service. I knew I wanted to personally thank people for coming, and I am so proud that my husband and our other two children could face all of those caring people too.

# Chapter 6

*Early May 2008*

Our family, including our dogs, experienced some wild ups and downs the weekend following the memorial service. A few days prior, we had already known what we'd be doing on Saturday, May 3. Pete, our second son, was the goalie for the Manasquan High School varsity lacrosse team, and he had missed only one game during our first week of grieving. A second game was postponed so that Pete's teammates could attend Tim's funeral service. Saturday was a big game for Manasquan High School, which is warmly known as "Squan." We encouraged Pete to play and decided quickly that we would attend too. We rarely miss a game and made an unspoken decision that today wouldn't be any different. We were going to watch Pete and cheer on the team as always. Andy and I gravitated to our usual places: Andy standing along the fence with the men and me sitting with some of the women. People around us were somewhat quiet and reserved, which I completely understood. Most of the families had already offered their condolences, either at our home or at the memorial service. One mom, who had stopped at the house, even asked me how she and others should act toward us at the upcoming game and my response was, "Try to treat us as normally as you can." I wasn't expecting a lot of small talk but, eventually, we chatted about the game itself.

At halftime we were down by five goals. As Peter's parents, we knew that he did not succumb to pressure, and that's why he made for a great goalkeeper. During the second half our team came back and miraculously won by one goal with very little time remaining. Several of the goals, including the winning one, were scored by Justin, a friend of Tim's. I happened to be sitting next to Justin's mom, Barbara. When the winning goal was scored, I turned to Barbara and asked, "Was that Justin?" and we both started crying and holding each other. I said it was definitely Tim who had brought victory to the team and helped Pete and Justin with the superb play that day. Barbara and others then stated that they had been thinking the same thing, but no one had wanted to say it out loud. I thanked God, and Tim, for such an uplifting moment.

When I woke up Sunday morning, May 4, I saw an empty eight-ounce box of mixed chocolates on the floor. Our house was still full of food and desserts, which had been gifts from visitors. We always have to keep the "people food" high enough so that our three dogs cannot reach it. After being greeted by Gordon, the puppy, and Blondie, our oldest dog, I looked around and then saw Ory lying unusually still and breathing quite heavily. I immediately called animal poison control. Based on Ory's weight, about eighty pounds, I was told that eight ounces of chocolate should not be a problem for him. We were warned that we should expect Ory to vomit and not feel well. Within an hour Ory's breathing seemed to be labored even more, and his stomach seemed so much more distended. I simply could not handle the worrying, and we decided to take him to the local animal hospital.

Watching Ory so sick, I found myself, for the first time, infuriated with Tim. I said to him, "You cannot have Ory! How dare you make him sick so that you can have one of our dogs with you!" I know this was a completely irrational reaction, and there have actually been very few occasions when I've been angry with Tim. Sadness, guilt, and emptiness far outweigh severe or even mild anger. But that day, I couldn't fathom having Pete and David suffer another significant loss so soon after Tim's death.

While Ory spent Sunday in the animal hospital, I took a bike ride by myself and began formulating a letter to the editor to send in to the *Coast Star*, our local weekly newspaper. I wanted to try to explain what had been going on with Tim. People seemed to have so many varying misconceptions: "He seemed so happy" and "I thought Tim was a good kid" to "No girl is worth this" to "Was he a drug addict?" to "Tim appeared to *have it all*" to "This is what happens when both parents work full time." And I don't even work full time!

I wanted to give concerned parents—as well as concerned kids, teachers, and members of my community—truthful answers from the person who knew him best, not guesses from those who were barely connected to him.

When I sat down the next morning to begin composing my letter, it took me very little time; the words just seemed to fall out of me. I explained that Tim was not a drug addict, at least not by definition—he was not *physically* dependent on any type of drug. I briefly described my sensitive child and my view of what had occurred during the last few months of our lives. Additionally, I tried to deliver two messages: 1) to encourage teens and young adults to turn to *people* for help, rather than substances, and 2) to ask all adults to try not to look the other way when it comes to teenage drinking and drug use. See Appendix A for the full letter.

For weeks after the letter was published my phones—both home and cell—did not stop ringing; nor did the emails stop pouring in. I wrote the letter to try to explain and to help others, but, in turn, I felt tremendously rewarded. I felt fulfilled that so many parents, kids, educators, and clergy seemed to benefit from my letter. The evening the letter was published, with the support of my friend Mary, I wrote to our principal to ask him if it would be appropriate to post the letter on the school web site. I later had some second thoughts, so the following morning, as I was leaving the principal a message apologizing for overstepping my bounds, the principal called me and expressed his complete approval. Many teachers were grateful to see the letter made available to all parents and students in our school community. Within a few weeks I received a letter from one of our congressional representatives thanking me for sharing and helping so many others.

One of the reactions to my letter expressed by people was, "I thought Tim was a good kid." Tim *was* a good kid. He was a wonderful son, my precious first-born child. He also was struggling with drugs. But I do not think Tim took his life *because* he was drinking and taking drugs. I believe his pain was so severe that the substances could no longer mask it.

Prior to Tim's death, I think I was somewhat judgmental toward people who use drugs *and* people who die by suicide. While I am still completely against underage drinking and all drug use, I now consider the multitude of reasons and the complexity of why some use and abuse drugs and alcohol, and inflict pain, or even death, upon themselves. Maybe this is why I am not comfortable with the phrase "committed suicide." After reading some of the self-help materials available for suicide survivors, I became more comfortable with and have settled into using the term "died by suicide." Maybe "died by suicide" allows me to think of the act as just another way someone dies, rather than focusing on the strength/power/ potency of the method.

My bike ride that Sunday not only helped me clear my head, but resulted in the first instance of my sharing my knowledge and feelings, to the best of my ability, in that letter. But perhaps the best news of the week was that Ory had his stomach pumped and by the next day he was released from the hospital and was back to being himself. Thank God.

# Chapter 7

Until Tim died I had thought of my life as divided into two segments: BC (Before Children) and AC (After Children). I do not claim to have invented these phrases BC and AC; I'm sure I'd heard them before. The segmentation into BC and AC came up for me frequently when trying to recall events that took place in my life when I was in my twenties and thirties, such as places I visited, music I listened to, people who were in my life at the time, and so much more. I had never really considered marriage as a major life change. Perhaps this was because Andy and I had been a couple for almost seven and a half years beforehand. We were minor acquaintances in high school, when we both attended Belleville High School in northern Jersey, but we began getting to know each other better while sitting together at a high school wrestling tournament just after Christmas in 1976. Andy was a college wrestler for Montclair State University at the time and had come to watch his old teammates as well as his brother, who was on the junior varsity team. I was a junior in high school just enjoying another wrestling match, which happened to be Belleville's number-one sport. It's somewhat prophetic that the two of us became attracted to each other at a school sporting event, since attending our boys' games has been a mainstay of our married life. Our interest in our children's activities, availability to drive them on demand, and openness to assisting them and supporting them in every way, have always come first. Not that we haven't had our share of conflicts regarding child rearing, but we have never disagreed on priority and commitment.

As for my life BC, I commuted to Montclair State University, only seven miles from Belleville. My Italian parents and maternal grandparents, who lived upstairs from us, believed that a girl should not leave home until she is married, including living on campus at college. As a sophomore in high school, I remember arguing about this issue. By the time I entered senior year, however, I was already serious with Andy, who also lived at home. Truthfully, the majority of my friends would be living at home and commuting to their schools as well. Belleville was filled with old-fashioned Italian families and was not an affluent area. There were numerous four-year colleges nearby, so many of us stayed at home and commuted to school during the day. Later, as adults, preparing to send our children away to college was therefore quite a new experience for Andy and me.

Andy and I share many common interests but our personalities are decidedly different. I do believe opposites attract. I like to talk, I'm extremely analytical, and I'm an obsessive planner. Andy is the type of person who talks about *real things*, meaning things that I consider important, only when he has something he needs to say, and he often says that "nothing" is on his mind. He can sometimes argue at length about a sports play or a referee's call, but I don't call those topics *real things*. Because I have known this about Andy for such a long time, his initial reaction to Tim's death was not surprising to me. As the years have passed, he has trusted me to make most of our plans. And honestly, most of our decisions—although not all of them—are made by me. At times, Andy may come across as uncaring, but I think it's more of a pattern we have comfortably fallen into, where I lead in most areas. This routine has worked for us over the years.

By the time I was twenty-eight, Andy and I had been married for more than four years and I had achieved my goal of being promoted to a systems manager at AT&T. I felt ready to have kids and I remember my first pregnancy as a wonderful time in my life. While I thought I wanted a girl, I felt that I was carrying a boy. I had always imagined a family of one boy and one girl or two girls. Three sons later it was clear that life hadn't turned out that way, but I have no regrets. Well, OK, most of the time I don't... Occasionally I still wish I had a daughter, but I would never consider trading in Tim, Pete, or Dave if given a second chance.

Through the years of raising my three sons, I continued to relate past events to life BC or life AC. Until Tim's death, that is. Since that time I have a new view of life segments: before Tim died and after Tim died. This new division is still very crisp. I feel acutely aware of whether each event from the past few years occurred before or after Tim died. While this is a much sadder division of life, it is the hard but real truth, and I have come to terms with it. The duration of my life before Tim died was almost forty-eight years. Things are different now, but I plan to do my best to enjoy my future years and to move forward with my hopes and dreams in the new segment of my life: after Tim's death.

# Part II

# Chapter 8

*1989–1994*

The due date for my first child was December 26, 1989. My first thought was that I was NOT allowing myself to have a Christmas baby. I sincerely believe that I willed myself to have the child early. As a fanatical planner, I was way ahead of myself for the upcoming holiday. I had completed all of my shopping and home decorating, and by December 7 we had purchased a live tree. The only holiday preparation I had left was to wrap the presents. I had found the perfect Christmas/birth announcement combination card, which read "A Baby and Christmas, Perfect Together." The cards were signed, and the envelopes were addressed and stamped. The only details remaining were filling out the birth announcement inserts and putting the cards in the mail.

Timothy Andrew Schenke arrived on December 9, nicely ahead of schedule, but not at all premature. Weighing six pounds eleven ounces and measuring nineteen inches long, Tim was absolutely perfect. Among the several "best days of my life" to date, this day tops them all. There is no other way to describe it, as I am sure most other moms will agree.

As Tim developed into a little person, it was easy to observe that he was a man of action rather than words. He walked extremely early, by the age of ten months, and his first word was "ball."

Tim was the first grandchild on both sides of the family, and as one might imagine, there was no shortage of love and attention. He grew into a happy, healthy, and extremely active toddler with a very strong will. Once, when Tim was about eighteen months old, Andy and I were riding bicycles with Tim strapped into a carrier on the back of Andy's bike. Thankfully, I was behind Andy because Tim found a way to wiggle himself free and actually stood up in the carrier. I remember yelling to Andy to pull over, but not too abruptly, for fear that Tim would be thrown from the bike.

Tim was an exceptionally late talker. When he was two years old, he had a small vocabulary of one syllable words and phrases. If Tim wanted something, he often said, "I wa…" and pointed without naming the item. When assessed for developmental delays the result was that he was just not ready to talk. We were relieved to be assured that he had no hearing problems or learning issues. On the contrary, Tim was extremely intelligent. At the age of two and a half, Tim could write out words, forming each letter of the alphabet nicely, but he could barely pronounce the simplest of them. I believe part of the issue was that Tim did not *want* to talk. For example, if I said, "You can't have the cup of milk until you say 'cup,'" he would just walk away. It seemed he would rather be thirsty than give in and try to say the word. From an early age this child had a mind of his own! He could not be persuaded with words, and truthfully, he could not be bribed with toys, snacks, or anything else. Between the ages of two and four and a half, Tim worked with three different speech therapists. The first therapist released Tim after a few months because she felt he had made appropriate progress. However, after the visits stopped, he seemed to plateau again. The second speech therapist played games with Tim; I specifically remember Chutes and Ladders. She and Tim appeared to have a personality clash. Because he possessed such a high intelligence level, I think this therapist expected more cooperation than Tim was capable of giving. The third was a charm, and before Tim entered kindergarten his speech was at or above grade level.

Our second child, Peter, was born just thirteen months after Tim. I think the rivalry started the day Pete came home from the hospital. Because Tim and Pete were both using pacifiers, I differentiated them by color. However, Tim quickly decided that Peter was not allowed to have a pacifier. Pete became a thumb-sucker instead because Tim always took the pacifier out of his mouth.

As Tim and Pete grew into toddlerhood together, it seemed they could not be more different. Pete was always interacting with people and loved attention. Tim had little regard for adults; he was just not interested in them or the attention they would give him. While Tim thoroughly enjoyed complex puzzles, it seemed Peter didn't want to waste his time on that level of minutia. Tim and Pete were also built entirely differently. Tim had a small build, while Pete has broad shoulders and a larger structure overall. When applying suntan lotion or giving the two of them a bath, Pete always seemed to have so much more area to cover. David came along in 1994, when Tim was four years old and Pete had just turned three. I felt almost immediately that David was a mixture of Tim and Pete in both looks and personality, and to this day he still is. Tim and Pete both seemed to like playing with David much more than they enjoyed interacting with each other. Theirs was a relationship of oil and water. This early conclusion continued to be accurate throughout their childhoods and adolescence.

Perhaps my strong will and determination to deliver my first baby early had somehow transferred to Tim, triggering him to become the strong-minded, resolute individual he was becoming.

# Chapter 9

*Early May 2008*

My largest area of concern during these early days of grieving, as well as today, was the impact of Tim's death on Pete and Dave. My concerns differed—concern for David because he and Tim were close, and concern for Pete because he and Tim were not.

Andy and I decided that Pete and David would go back to school after being home for one week, but we would not return to work until the following week, mainly so that we could be there for the kids if they were having problems. Roughly six years before Tim's death, I had made a career change and began working part-time as a personal fitness trainer. My clients were very understanding, and I was able return in phases. It seemed that Pete and David took turns with who was struggling. Just before the funeral, David had become physically sick. After attending just one day of school, Pete had a headache, body aches, and felt a complete loss of concentration. Because both boys were in spring sports—Pete played high school lacrosse and David elementary school tennis—they did not want to miss school. I found this to be a tremendous motivator for them to get out the door each day. I took Peter to our family doctor, who gave us a great suggestion. He wrote a note stating that Pete could spend as much time as necessary in the nurse's office as long as he was getting his schoolwork done. This situation worked well for the month of May, and by June, Pete was back in class full-time.

The second week, just as Andy and I were returning to work, it seemed to be David's turn again. David was having such difficulty sleeping that he struggled to get up in the morning. One day, after David's English teacher observed him crying while trying to do some individual desk work in her class, she called me to ask me to come get him. I believe it was harder for him to control his emotions while continuously sleep-deprived. I took the advice of a friend and worked out an arrangement with the school that allowed David to go in late every day as long as he was making up the work. I was able to drive David to school when I was between clients, and the teachers were wonderfully understanding and helpful. I also suggested the nurse's office as an option for David, but David was not fond of the elementary school nurse. We settled on the vice principal's office as a resting place for David when he needed to leave the classroom.

During this period of time, I remember David asking me, "What if I can't remember Tim's voice?" Tim's intonation reflected his personality. It was neither loud nor pitchy, which might indicate an extrovert. He had more of an even, fast, and quiet tone, maybe indicative of a quick-thinking but shy individual. I believe I responded to David, "Of course we won't forget his voice, and we always have the camcorder," but then I cried for days contemplating that thought.

# Chapter 10

*1991–1995*

Tim was a highly active but at times fearful toddler. Before moving to the Jersey Shore in 1999, we owned a thirty-foot travel trailer that we would use on weekends and during the summer. It had two very small bedrooms, a kitchen table that converted to a bed, and a sofa bed. At only eight feet wide, it was tight, but we got by just fine, spending as little time indoors as possible. We would anchor it in a kid-friendly campground near Long Beach Island, close to two hours from our home in Middlesex, New Jersey, and about forty-five minutes south of where we live now. The campground had a pool, playground, candy store, and unfortunately, lots of greenheads, which are flies that bite. It was close to the Pinelands, a heavily wooded area of New Jersey, filled with pine and cedar trees. We enjoyed many weekends there, driving a short distance to the beach in Surf City or swimming in Barnegat Bay. Because Tim did not enjoy the feeling of sand between his toes, he chose to keep his socks and sneakers on. I think it was his third summer when he eventually started allowing us to take his sneakers off when he left the blanket, just a little at a time. We also went to various New Jersey oceanfront boardwalks on Saturday nights, including Seaside Heights, Ocean City, Wildwood, and Cape May. I clearly recall Tim and Pete wanting to shake hands with Mr. Peanut out in front of the Planters Peanut store in Ocean City. We have wonderful memories of those ten summers in southern Ocean County. My parents also owned a trailer that they parked in the same campground, so we often had help running after the three energetic boys.

The campground held an annual Halloween party at the end of September, just before the end-of-season shutdown. Tim was extremely afraid of the haunted hayride, but we were able to persuade him to go on the first ride of the night. The younger children were encouraged to go on the early rides because as the night became darker, the ride became scarier. Tim was also very sensitive to loud noises and cautious of any type of surprise. I am a big fan of fireworks, and I can remember some instances where a family member had to take Tim to the car or into a nearby arcade because he was so unhappy with the sound and the vibration. Along those same lines, I also remember Tim wearing a scarf over his ears when we went to see the TV character Barney in concert in New York City.

Because Tim was born on December 9 and the cutoff date for kindergarten was October 31, Tim was unable to start school at the same time as the others he had been grouped with in the small local preschool. To remedy that, I moved him to a larger prekindergarten environment where I felt there would be more children his age and he would fit in better academically. Tim was very bright and tended to fidget and move around when he was not challenged. Two months after Tim entered kindergarten the following year, I asked the teacher and school administration about moving him up a grade. I was told that was only done in very rare circumstances, and all aspects of Tim's performance would have to be stellar. While Tim definitely possessed the intelligence, he was not ready behaviorally. For example, he moved around on the carpet during circle time. Tim's activity level was very high, both at school and at home. He sometimes seemed to be running on a nonstop motor, as if he was unable to calm himself down. Tim was always *on the go* at home. He would often see how far he could slide across the kitchen floor, which drove me absolutely nuts and caused me to shout at him. When involved in physical activities, Tim was always drawn to risk—

so opposite of the fearful and shy boy who disliked unfamiliar settings, noises, and sensations.

# Chapter 11

Self-soothing was a difficult but necessary act for me. Being home alone was often the biggest challenge. Because I work part-time, primarily between 6:00 AM and noon with minimal clients in the evening, I am often home alone during the afternoons. Before Tim's death, I used to cherish every moment of that time. Living in a loud household with four males, the TV would always be blasting and the one-upsmanship involved in male conversations (I call them arguments, but they call them "conversations") would always be going on. Now here I was, feeling almost ill being alone in the silent house.

The dark, gray days were the hardest, and these were the days I would cry the most. I am definitely a person who requires sunlight. At first I avoided the gym and only exercised on days I could go outside, but within a short time I was back at the gym. I had also avoided the grocery store, pharmacy, and all the other local places where I'd run into people, but I knew I had to return there also and soon did. Sometimes I would actually see people turning their carts and avoiding contact with me because it was so awkward for them. Believe me, it was awkward for me too. Some days the other person would be crying and I just wasn't in a crying place at that moment. It felt very strange when an outsider was crying for my loss and I was not.

One of the places that I unexpectedly found comfort was in the Rosary. When Father Brian gave the four of us—Andy, Pete, David, and me—each a set of rosary beads, I told him that I had never learned how to pray with them. He gave me a thick book, but the basic directions could be found on the first few pages. I turned to those rosary beads at times when I just did not know what else to do with myself, when nothing felt right. This was new and strange for me. I often felt that because I am not a regular churchgoer and do not pray regularly, I shouldn't pray just when I needed something. Regardless of whether I was praying the Rosary, or just saying the three prayers I knew from childhood, the repetition would somehow calm me. I regret that my children don't know my three prayers; most likely they can recall only the one that we had practiced, the "Our Father."

I was raised Catholic and my husband was raised Presbyterian. We had agreed to raise our kids in some type of Christian church, but in the long run, it seemed that neither of us really took ownership or leadership in attending services regularly or enforcing Sunday school after the first few years. Now, in a time of crisis when I would have liked my kids to turn to religion, I could suggest it—and I did—but I did not feel that I had the right to demand it or to shove it down their throats. I have often worried about Tim lacking a strong religious upbringing too. What is even more concerning to me is whether or not he had faith. In retrospect, I would have raised the boys Catholic even though Andy had said he would not convert; not because I feel they must be Catholic in their adult lives, but because they would have had a solid foundation in Christianity. In addition, the families in the two towns we had lived in were largely Catholic, so it would have been easy to send them to religion classes where many of their friends were going.

Listening to music has always been something I've turned to for comfort. It can be such a gauge of how I am feeling. I have always been one to listen to music on the radio when I'm alone in the car. However, listening to music was now a nearly impossible task. Each song brought up so many emotions that I often drove the car in silence. For example, I used to sing along with "Bohemian Rhapsody" by Queen without giving much thought to the words. Now I could not tolerate hearing the line,

"Momma, life had just begun, but now I've gone and thrown it all away." I also encountered so many songs that we enjoyed together and songs that I would try to explain to the kids. I guess I sometimes repeated my explanations, and I can remember Tim rolling his eyes and saying, "You already told me." I specifically recall describing the meaning of "I Hope You Dance" by LeAnn Rimes, which Tim later used in an English project when he was in ninth grade.

We are big fans of the TV show *American Idol*, and we did return to watching the final episodes after a week or two away from the show. I had loved one of the contestants, David Cook, from the very beginning. Andy and I both remember Tim just popping in and sitting on the couch while eating a snack. He was not a fan, but would add a few comments, or more likely insults, here and there. While watching those episodes, I would sometimes look at his seat on the couch and expect to see him. Then the sad reality would hit me.

When David Cook won in late May, the song he sang was "Time of My Life." As I was beginning to listen to the radio again, I felt a jolt of positive feeling whenever I would hear this song. I made a decision to allow those feelings, and I still think of this song as my return to enjoying music. The song referenced *tasting every moment and living it out loud*, which I thought was a great message. Since I had been trying to be as upbeat and positive as possible with Pete and David, I began repeating the words to myself as an affirmation. When planning a special event to celebrate life at the first anniversary of Tim's death about nine months later, this song served as a strong motivator for me. I focused on the message of "embrace life" as I planned and promoted the gathering to honor Tim's memory.

Another solace, perhaps the most important during this time, was grief counseling. Our family doctor referred us to David Cotton, a grief counselor at the local hospital. Andy and I met with David C. first, and I immediately felt a connection to him. David C., as I will affectionately refer to him, encouraged each of us to work with him individually; he explained that couples grieve in different ways and recover at different rates. While I began seeing David C. for weekly counseling, Andy saw him every two or three weeks. After insisting that Pete and David try it, they both stopped after a few sessions. As teenage boys, it was no surprise

39

that they did not want to go and David C. told us that it was not worth trying to force them if they were not ready. They both seemed to be functioning well and did not appear to be in emotional danger.

David C. has been a tremendous support to me. I do not feel that I could have gotten to where I am now without him. During the early visits, David C. would say to me, "When you are feeling good, please allow yourself to feel it. It's so important to stay with the positive for as long as you can." David C. carefully explained and strongly persuaded me to *allow* the good feelings to exist. He indicated that pushing them away would not help me in progressing through my grief. Taking that advice was difficult; it didn't feel good to be depressed, but it almost felt worse to be happy. It was most comfortable to feel just medium, not too high or too low, because after the highs, the lows always felt debilitating. Fortunately, with time, I did learn to accept, and even enjoy, the highs.

# Chapter 12

In certain ways, Tim was a leader. He liked to be first in line and to engage others in active play such as running and jumping. But in other ways he was bashful and introverted. Even though Tim was one of the most intelligent and athletic boys in his school, he was often insecure about trying new things and about speaking up for himself. When spring of kindergarten year arrived, he refused to participate in Little League T-ball because he thought he wasn't good enough. We disagreed and tried to encourage him because we knew he was one of the most agile boys in his grade. Although he did not play, he joined the following year when he and Peter were both eligible, and he turned out to be one of the most skilled hitters and fielders in the league.

Sitting in a chair for a full day of school as a first-grader proved to be challenging for Tim. But no matter how much he fidgeted, talked, got up to sharpen his pencil, and sucked his sleeve, he could still score practically a 100 on every test or quiz, which only frustrated his first-grade teacher more. She referred Tim to a Pupil Assistance Committee (PAC) and we soon had Tim assessed for Attention Deficit Hyperactivity Disorder (ADHD). I had already read up on ADHD because I was well aware of Tim's hyperactive traits. Tim was not diagnosed with ADHD because, even though he did possess many of the impulsive and hyperactive characteristics, he was not suffering any consequences academically or socially. In addition, asking for extra time to complete assignments or tests was completely unnecessary because he was often the first one done, with minimal errors. The doctors agreed that there was no reason to medicate Tim; the teacher would just have to deal with it. Second grade was a much more pleasant experience. The second-grade teacher gave Tim extra responsibilities and sometimes sent him to the library to work on enrichment projects with two other students.

I remember a frustrating day at church when Tim was in second grade. This was during a period when we had joined a Methodist church. Normally the children would attend the first part of the service with their parents then, immediately after the children's sermon, they would leave for Sunday school. One Sunday, Tim stayed in church with us because he was tired. Tim and Pete were in the same Sunday school class at that time. On our way home that day Pete told us that the teacher asked where Tim was. When Pete explained that he was staying in church with the adults, she said something like, "Good, then I won't have to deal with him." I responded that she had no right to say that. I recall being angry at the teacher's comment on two levels: first, adults should not talk about children in this manner; and second, this kind of talk should not happen in front of other children. As a result, my child was now hearing this criticism about his brother and then passing it on to him. I don't think Pete meant to insult Tim, but I can imagine that this incident, along with other similar incidents, contributed to Tim's low opinion of himself. I never did speak to this teacher or to the person in charge of Sunday school, and I regret that. I can't remember exactly, but I think I decided against it because, unlike school, this was only one hour per week so we would just "make do" with the situation.

By the middle of third grade we were back to different doctors, again evaluating Tim for ADHD and receiving similar feedback. As a parent, I was both relieved and stressed by the lack of a diagnosis. I was glad Tim did not need medication, but on the other hand, we still had a lot to deal with on a day-to-day basis, both at home and in school. In first grade, Tim's teacher along with Andy and I utilized a reward system involving smiley faces. Tim's third-grade teacher was a lot less structured and didn't believe in formal behavior management.

What I took away from Tim's first through third grade experience was the following: I learned to request the most structured, patient, and academically innovative teacher—if such an individual existed. I am pleased to say that Tim did not lose interest in schoolwork and continued to participate and raise his hand in class, even though teachers couldn't call on him every time, which he sometimes found frustrating. Because Tim exhibited hyperactivity and impulsivity, *and* he evidenced low self-esteem, we started him in counseling during third grade. The counselor's opinion on whether to medicate Tim was 50-50. After another thorough discussion with our family physicians, they once again recommended against it based on how well Tim functioned. The counselor shared that he did not think Tim was depressed, rather that he was manipulative. I didn't really agree with "manipulative"—I thought Tim often acted *before* thinking due to his extreme impulsivity.

While Tim was energetic all day, he had the most energy in the mornings. In elementary school he always got up first and watched a sports channel on TV to find out about the previous night's games. While Pete and David needed to be continually prodded to get ready for school on time, Tim always had too much extra time, which often meant running around the house and riling up the other two. Tim's second-grade teacher suggested that we try giving Tim a can of Coke in the morning, a stimulant that sometimes has the reverse effect on children. It seemed to have no effect one way or the other. I remember wishing that school started earlier so the disciplining wouldn't have to start before we even left for work in the morning. I didn't feel good going to work after yelling at Tim, and then I worried about the impact on him too. But, people would tell me, "Kids are resilient." Looking back now, if given the chance to do it all again, I would have tried to act positively more of the time.

Now that all three of our children had evolved from toddlers to early grade-schoolers, we became much more mobile and developed various outdoor family traditions. We thoroughly enjoyed apple picking, pumpkin picking, navigating mazes, climbing lighthouses, and walking on jetties at the beach. We also selected a Christmas tree from a tree farm each year and dug it out of the ground ourselves. As all parents know, along with the fun times come some conflicts, especially with three boys close in age. Pete was often a pest to Tim, and Tim would lose his patience and respond physically. The outcome was that they were often both punished because each of them would say, "He started it." Punishment needs to be something that works for that particular child. Tim always liked to be first, to be in the front. An effective consequence for him was to have him walk in the back with Dad because Dad usually walked the slowest.

With the exception of David, we all had our conflicts with Tim. Andy coached Tim's traveling soccer teams, grades two through five, two years in each of the two different towns we lived in. Andy has also coached recreational sports, but travel is more intense because it is a more serious level of competition and tends to be year-round. Tim and Andy had their share of head-butting, as do many fathers and sons in this position. From my viewpoint, most fathers who coach their sons tend to be either too easy or too harsh with their own child. I feel that Andy was too harsh with Tim, which caused Tim to rebel even more. Tim ran plenty of laps at practice, but he would continue to mouth off. Once again, I believe it was a matter of impulse control. When Tim was entering sixth grade, he moved to a higher-level team, coached by others, and this was a relief to us all.

We frequently played miniature golf as a family and Tim was the sorest loser in the group. He would often stop trying when the game was not going his way. Along those same lines, I can recall a silent burst of anger after an inconsequential Little League baseball game. When the last out for our team was called, Tim immediately tore off his uniform shirt because he was so disgusted with the loss.

As the years passed, I thought to myself that Tim inherited the hardest traits from his parents and other relatives; he somehow acquired the most difficult-to-live-with genes from the gene pool. Seriousness and perfectionism from me. Competitiveness and minimal verbal expression from Andy. And anger, fear, and impulsivity from a variety of his relatives.

Most people are surprised to hear that we do not have any history of alcoholism or drugs in our families. We do, however, have some relatives with gambling problems and eating disorders, which also qualify as addictive behaviors. I suffered from an eating disorder and became too thin during my college years and into my twenties. I still tend to be a control freak; but I did learn, with time, that it wasn't about the food or the size of my body. Although Pete and Dave have their quirks, like everyone does, thankfully they seem to have escaped receiving the complex mixture of genes that Tim possessed.

Not only was David a combination of Tim and Pete, halfway between them in looks and personality, but he could also get along well with each of them, one at a time. At times, when it was just the three of them, Tim and Pete would almost argue over David, each trying to get him to play.

When given the choice, David would choose Tim. Whenever something came up that required pairs, such as two-seater rides, two people on the same side of a booth, etc., Tim and David paired up. Most of the time, Peter didn't even mind. Pete was always the most independent and outgoing of the three, often willing to sit alone or meet someone new.

David seemed to idolize Tim throughout the years and frequently took Tim's number for sports. When Tim started playing traveling soccer at the age of eight, he chose number twenty-four, for New York Yankees player Tino Martinez. As soon as David was old enough to start playing, he also chose number twenty-four. A few years later, when David was interviewed by a reporter for the elementary school newspaper, he was asked who his idol was and he responded, "My brother Tim."

# Chapter 13

Pete made some quick decisions in the weeks immediately following Tim's death. Just a few months earlier, we had helped Peter purchase a used yellow Saturn Vue. The bright yellow SUV seemed to fit Pete's personality. He was comfortable with the attention drawn by driving a brightly colored car. Although the car had over 100,000 miles it had been well maintained and looked relatively new.

When Tim had turned seventeen years old, he bought a used Honda Accord. Tim was a good saver. Beginning with about a thousand dollars from his eighth grade graduation, he had saved seven thousand dollars total by working at Hoffman's Ice Cream. He knew exactly what type of car he wanted, and it seemed to match his personality. It was a black four-door sedan, a very under the radar, common car; perfect for a kid who did not like to be noticed. Although we were already battling with Tim about alcohol and pot, we were proud of how much money he had saved. When he found this car, and it wiped his saving clean, we decided to provide the sixteen-hundred-dollar balance needed for him to secure the purchase.

After Tim's death, we offered Pete the choice of keeping his car or Tim's car, expecting him to keep his own. He surprised us by choosing

Tim's car. He said it was the better car, which is probably true, but we think he really wanted to keep that piece of Tim. After Pete made that decision, I was kind of sorry we had offered a choice at all because I did not like having Tim's car around. When we got the car cleaned up, I asked Pete if he still wanted the Drexel University sticker, the school Tim was planning to attend, on the back window and he said, "I guess not." Looking at that car without the sticker hurt me for quite a long time, but I didn't dwell on it in front of Pete.

A short time later, Pete followed in Tim's footsteps and began working at Hoffman's Ice Cream. I also think that was part of Pete's wanting to experience another area of Tim's life. When Tim was alive, I had strongly expressed that we did not want Pete to apply for a job there. The two of them were always at odds at home and I thought they did not need to bring that into the workplace. Since Hoffman's was Tim's "thing," Pete should not apply there. Tim had wholeheartedly agreed with me on that, but now he was gone, and my second son put on a Hoffman's shirt.

These issues of what to keep the same and what to change in the wake of Tim's death were a constant. I had been reading several books on grieving to get some advice on this issue. Each book suggested changing everyone's seats at the kitchen table, but we didn't. Yes, the empty seat was painful, but Andy and I agreed that it seemed so artificial to change it.

What no amount of reading prepared me for was the worst question a grieving mom has to face: "How many children do you have?" My answer has varied over the years from, "Had three, have two now" to "Had three, but one died…" to "Two" to "Three." I usually just say, "Three" and take it from there depending on who the other person is, my mood, and maybe the constellations or something cosmic that day.

Our first time out to dinner as a family after Tim's death was on May 19, which was our twenty-fourth wedding anniversary. It was unbelievably awkward for our reduced family to enter a restaurant together. As the waitress approached, she said, "Party of four," and I seriously wanted to shoot daggers at her because the sting was so severe. Our conversation began to flow, and eventually I asked Pete and David if they wanted to place Tim's ashes into the ocean that evening. During the first week after Tim's death we did not jump into any decision about the ashes. I had always told Andy that I wanted my ashes to be poured into the ocean, and he typically said, "Whatever you want to do with me is fine." I had previously mentioned this to Pete and David, and they said they really didn't care. As to the question of distributing the ashes tonight, David said, "When I die, I don't want to go into the ocean, I want to go underground; not into a drawer either, only underground." That was quite definitive, so I next asked David if he preferred that Tim go into the ground, and I believe he answered that he didn't know. At that moment, I suggested that I could change my plan to scatter Tim's ashes into the ocean if that's what Pete and David preferred. Everyone seemed to accept that, so on to a new plan. My parents were relieved. I had been ignoring their request for a burial because I felt strongly that Andy, Pete, and David were the only ones who should have any input on this topic. Almost immediately, Andy and I began working on the new plan for Tim's burial. Andy's paternal grandparents had retired to northern Ocean County, only about fifteen minutes south of our home, years before their deaths. Because they are buried in Greenwood Cemetery, approximately halfway between their old home and our current home, we chose the same cemetery. Surprisingly, there was space available right next to the family plot. It hadn't looked like it because the cremation-size plots are only half plots. We now felt a sense of connection to the cemetery and I became more accepting of the new plan.

# Chapter 14

*1999–2000*

Our family moved one hour southeast, from Middlesex, New Jersey to Spring Lake Heights in June 1999. We had hoped the move would go smoothly for the boys, and for the most part it did. I had always wanted to live closer to the ocean, and the right job opportunity had come along for Andy. I would telecommute for my job most days and travel the hour back to the office approximately once per week. I had always known that if we were to move, we would do so before the boys became teenagers. I felt that at the ages of nine, eight, and five they would adjust easily. The night before we left Middlesex, Tim had planned to sleep over at his friend Carl's house, but during that evening Carl's mom called and said Tim wanted to come home. When we picked him up, he said he wanted to sleep in his own house for the last time. The day of the move, my parents came to the house to help us out. The plan was for the boys to go to the Seaside Heights boardwalk, not far from our new house, with their grandparents and to meet us at the house later. Because Tim refused to go with Grandma and Grandpa, Pete and David refused too. We listened to their needs and allowed them to ride in the car with us after the moving truck was loaded and on the road. The movers were a group of young guys who ended up playing Wiffle ball in the yard with the kids at our new home, which really helped.

The summer recreation program in Spring Lake Heights started in early July each year. The program was open to children entering kindergarten through eighth grade, and at the time Tim was going into fourth grade, Pete into third grade, and David into kindergarten. On the first day, Andy and I decided to take the boys together as a family. Tim, who was generally reluctant about meeting new people and trying new things, needed a push. Pete jumped right in, and David slowly joined in on the appropriate activities for his age group. The personality traits exhibited here seemed to appear again and again as the years went by. When Tim came to sit with us, we told him that he had to go back and play with the boys. We stayed in view for the remainder of the morning. Sure enough, by the time the three hours passed, Tim was having a great time too, which was often the case after he was pressed to try something new.

Tim made a best friend that summer, Mark. However, when the class assignments for fourth grade arrived in the mail in late August, Mark was not in Tim's class; nor were the other two primary boys he had become friendly with. Tim cried in bed at night a few times during those first few weeks of school when I would lie with him before he went to sleep. He felt that the kids did not like him. I tried to reassure him that it wasn't that they didn't like him, it was just that they didn't know him yet. I was confident that as an athletic, intelligent boy, he would be easily accepted.

Based on Tim being a sensitive child and some prior displays of low self-esteem, I decided to find a therapist for him and brought him a handful of times. Tim did adjust and soon returned to his accustomed popularity. I don't really know if it was help from the therapist or just a matter of time, but I was happy about it either way.

Tim's fourth-grade teacher, Mr. York, was the first male teacher he had ever had. I think the relationship was positive, and I remained in close contact with him. Mr. York did notice Tim's hyperactive and impulsive traits, and they worked through them, although Tim did not like being punished for talking or getting out of hand in class. The schoolwork was becoming a little more challenging, especially with a change in curriculum due to our move to a different school district. However, Tim did very well and achieved all A's as he had previously. Mr. York once told me that Tim often stood at his desk while taking tests instead of sitting. He had no problem with that and allowed Tim to stand and lean over the desk to complete the tests. By this age Tim was aware of his "borderline ADHD" as we referred to it. Tim knew that although he had difficulty with calling out answers, waiting his turn, and other hyperactive behaviors, he was responsible for his actions. Tim understood and accepted that I would explain his personality to his teachers and they would help where possible, but ultimately he was accountable for what went on in class.

I always thought I had the memory of an elephant, and until Tim was ten or eleven years old, he and I were competitive about remembering things. Whether it was trying to remember the name of a street, or a locker combination, or any small detail, we enjoyed our rivalry. Honestly, by the time Tim was a teenager he had far surpassed me. I guess it was a combination of Tim's becoming sharper with age and my getting into my forties. Once, when Tim was in a high school math class, the teacher offered extra credit to the student who could memorize the most digits of the decimal pi (3.14159…). Tim did not study, but only looked at the numbers on the blackboard for a day or two during class. Having memorized about twenty digits, Tim came in second place because another student memorized more digits by studying at home.

Tim and I had some great talks in the dark in his bed. These talks continued into high school, maybe ending around ninth grade. This particular year, during fourth grade, Tim had a few realizations that made him feel sad. That December, Tim was complaining day after day that he was too old to believe in Santa Claus. How could I treat him like a baby when all the other kids knew Santa was not real? I finally gave in and admitted the truth, but I told him he could not ruin it for Pete and David. That same night, about a half hour after our discussion in his bed, he came to the stairs crying because he was sad that Santa wasn't real. Needless to say, I was so angry with myself for giving in to his pressuring me.

At this time in Tim's life, he wanted to be a professional basketball player and to first play for Duke University. Sometimes, when he voiced this to others, he told me he would receive feedback that realistically he would probably never play for Duke because he was too short, among other reasons. When we talked about it, I tried to remain positive but not unrealistic. I think I said it would be very difficult, but it was too early to tell and he should continue to work on all the sports he enjoyed. One night while lying in his room, Tim became upset over his own realization that he would never play basketball for Duke. Tim was mature for his age, and he sometimes preferred to hang around with older boys. However, he felt things deeply and did not possess the confidence to match that maturity, or the confidence one might expect for such an academically and athletically capable child.

Amber, a friend of Tim's who is the sister of Logan and Ashley, became Tim's first steady girlfriend during fourth grade. At that time, Tim did not have a cell phone, and I can vividly remember him sitting around waiting for Amber to call or to call him back. Tim was the type of child who was serious and committed to the task at hand, be it a sports competition, a dare to jump off a garage roof, or a girl. I can also remember Tim becoming upset over the love triangle developing with Amber and his friend Mark. Within a few months the romance was over, but fortunately all remained friends. Additionally, Tim remained close to Logan, Amber's brother, throughout elementary and high school.

I believe it was later this same year that Timothy Andrew Schenke became known as Tim, rather than Timmy. I have referred to him as Tim throughout this book because I cannot imagine calling him Timmy again. Unlike my other two children whom I call Peter and Pete, David and Dave, Tim is just Tim.

# Chapter 15

B ack at home we never knew when we would have a busy evening or a quiet evening. People still stopped by, but with less regularity. Teenagers would tend to stop by late at night, sometimes after I was already dozing on the couch. Some friends, especially Tim's friend Logan, would ask to spend a few minutes in Tim's room. A few people had suggested that I either keep a window open or a light on so that Tim's spirit could visit his room whenever he chose to.

While roaming around my favorite little downtown, Point Pleasant, New Jersey, one afternoon, I found a starfish nightlight that I thought would be perfect for Tim's room. It's a lot brighter than an average nightlight, but not as overwhelming as a lamp. It was just right. On one of Logan's visits, I walked into David's room while Logan and David were listening to a song from Tim's iPod, crying together. I have to admit that I was shocked when Logan asked me if he could hold the urn that contained Tim's ashes. The urn had been in a bag in Tim's room, hidden away. Why not? I guess there would be no harm done, so they followed me to Tim's room. Logan hugged the urn for a long time and then encouraged David to hold it too. It's unbelievable that each time I thought I couldn't feel any more raw or vulnerable, some other situation would pop up. My heart was breaking, but I also felt such affection for Logan and the way he tried to take care of David.

I specifically remember two early visits that sort of honored Tim. One evening two friends representing Tim's Advanced Placement calculus class came to visit—Kevin W., who was both a classmate and a soccer friend, and Madeline, who was a classmate Tim had been close to all four years of high school. I had never met Madeline before, but I had written her a note thanking her for putting up pictures of academic memories on Tim's Facebook memorial page. Madeline had added pictures from AP calculus, National Honor Society, and study period in the library. Kevin W. and Madeline presented us with a shirt that had been designed by the class and worn on the day of the final AP calculus exam. Tim was still alive when the shirt was designed in mid-April. The exam took place on May 8. At the time the design had been finalized, Tim had announced that he was going to cut the sleeves off because he wanted a sleeveless shirt. When exam day came around, the entire class wore their shirts to school with the sleeves cut off. They also autographed Tim's shirt, the one that was presented to us by Kevin W. and Madeline that night at our house.

Numerous blank paper banners had been hung throughout the school to allow students to express their thoughts to Tim. When taken down a few days later, they were given to me. I hung them up in Tim's bedroom for a month or so, reading them over and over. Many visitors to my home appreciated reading the kind words and memories too. I asked Madeline what the "Schenke Dynasty" meant because I had seen it mentioned in her note to Tim on one of the banners. Madeline explained that Tim often told the calc class that he wanted eight kids, and they would become the "Schenke Dynasty." He had also shared that one of the eight would be named Frank Schenke after Grandpa Frank, my father. I don't think I ever knew that Tim wanted such a large family. I was so surprised that I have to wonder if it was it the truth or perhaps an exaggeration? Maybe Tim felt he wanted so many children because of his love for David? Maybe he really did feel closeness to Pete even though the two of them almost never showed it? Is it possible that Tim knew that our lives revolved around our kids and we loved it that way, and therefore he wanted even more?

On another evening, the soccer coaches—the head varsity coach, two assistants, the junior varsity coach, and the freshman coach—all arrived together to present us with a beautiful blown-up black-and-white photo of Tim and a video of a game from his senior season. Coach Levy, the head varsity coach, also told us that number six would be retired: No other player would be allowed to wear that number for as long as he was around to make sure of it. Another beautiful memory regarding number six involves Rob, a slightly older soccer friend of Tim's who changed his college soccer number to six in honor of Tim. Rob played for Kean College in New Jersey, and we later enjoyed watching him play at a few of his home games and maintained an ongoing friendship. I had been told that the soccer coaches had gotten together with the players a few times to check on them. They were such caring individuals who later offered kind words and ongoing support to Pete and David too.

# Chapter 16

*2001–2004*

During Tim's preteen and early teenage years, I feel that he really blossomed. Excelling at middle-school sports, building more mature and solid friendships with both boys and girls, and seeming to gain the confidence to more easily accept new experiences really helped Tim. He appeared to be more comfortable in his own skin.

Our family shared a great California vacation when Tim, Pete, and David were in fifth, fourth, and first grades. A new Disney amusement park, California Adventure, had just recently opened. Tim and Pete both went on an upside-down roller coaster with full loops for the first time in their lives. Just like when they started playing Little League, Tim waited for Pete to be ready. With Little League, Tim finally agreed to join when Peter became old enough to play. Now Tim was waiting for Pete to be tall enough to ride the upside-down coaster. Tim was so proud of that accomplishment! The previous fall, he had gone to our local amusement park with some boys his age who were already going on those types of coasters. He was so happy he'd be riding with them the next time they went together.

As a sixth-grader, Tim was a starter on the middle-school soccer team, which is a big accomplishment, and he scored in the first game.

Seventh-grade girls started calling him that night. The middle-school environment, within the Spring Lake Heights Elementary School, was a great fit for Tim. The school was small enough for Tim's soccer skills to allow him to become a valued player in sixth grade, and the freedom to change classes for every subject made school much more interesting for him. It also gave him the opportunity to walk in the halls rather than sit at one desk for long periods of time. In addition, the vice principal began to develop a relationship with Tim, which I believe encouraged him to become a leader and a role model. I think it was also around this time that Tim became known for his smile. When asked today, "What do you think of first when you think of Tim?" the most common response is, "His smile."

Tim also played on the junior varsity basketball team, composed of sixth- and seventh-graders who tried out and made the team. I strongly believe that the increased activity of playing school sports every afternoon, as well as being able to move around during the school day, benefitted Tim greatly both in school and at home. I feel he was able to relax a little more at home rather than having to let off so much excess steam. One of my fondest memories of Tim was the two of us lying on the loveseat together watching TV when he'd come home and squeeze in next to me. We both wanted the inside, but I would give in and let him have the better spot.

While Tim continued to excel, he still disliked being the center of attention. When the kids were younger, we usually celebrated their birthdays at a restaurant where the waiters would sing and make a big fuss over the birthday child. Tim used to hide his eyes or try to crawl under the table when it was his birthday celebration. As a young teen, and as a member of the school baseball team in seventh and eighth grades, Tim enjoyed playing the field much more than being up at bat. If Tim had two strikes on him, he would often just strike out. He just did not have the patience or the confidence to wait out the pitches. Pete was completely the opposite; when faced with a full count, he often had his best hits.

Tim told me he wished he could be a designated fielder and wondered why teams had designated hitters but not designated fielders. He was an excellent outfielder who had both the agility to get to the ball, and the strength and accuracy to throw to home plate. I can actually remember the throw to home plate becoming an issue once or twice with a Little League coach. The coach expected Tim to throw to the shortstop or cutoff man. However, Tim wanted to make his own decisions about when to throw to home plate because he knew he could do it.

During the summer of 2003, when Tim was going into eighth grade, we vacationed in Bar Harbor, Maine, at Acadia National Park. Some of the climbing was too risky for me, but Tim was always in the lead, never having to slow down to catch his breath. I often thought that I should have started Tim in gymnastics or some extreme-sports-challenge type of activity when he was younger because he had such balance and agility. I also remember allowing Tim to use his cell phone for a few minutes each night on our Maine vacation to talk to a female friend who he claimed was not his girlfriend despite all the time he spent with her, both in person and on the phone. The minutes were precious because that was before the days of free roaming and night and weekend minutes. Tim anxiously awaited his opportunity to make that call each evening.

As an eighth-grader, Tim was chosen to be captain of the soccer team and of the varsity basketball team. He was also selected as a peer leader. Although Tim was reluctant to volunteer or try out for visible positions, he did seem to enjoy and excel at it, and felt proud when selected. When it came time to choose a high school, I urged Tim to take the test for one of the specialty county high schools for high-performing students, but Tim refused. In the end I did force Tim to take the test for the local Catholic high school. Tim's performance on the test was average, and he informed me that he would not earn better than a "C" in each subject if I made him attend. Anyone who knew Tim would know that he was not bluffing. He was strong-willed and would not be persuaded or bribed. Tim did agree to take honors classes at the local Manasquan High School.

My primary reason for wanting Tim to attend a specialty county school or the local Catholic school was because they were smaller. Based on how well Tim fit into the Spring Lake Heights middle school environment, I sincerely believed a smaller school, where the administration might know him, stay on top of him, and give him some pats on the back would be beneficial. After Tim's death, Mark, the close friend of Tim's who was his best friend that first summer in Heights, told me that Tim did not read the questions when he took the admissions test for the Catholic high school. Instead, he randomly went down the answer sheet checking off A, C, D, C—as in AC/DC, the popular rock band. Well, that explained why he had achieved only mediocre results on the admissions test. But he had still passed!

Throughout eighth grade Tim seemed to be at the top of his game. In addition to the responsibilities of peer leader and team captain for two sports, Tim also performed specific leadership duties for the vice principal on the eighth grade class trip. Tim seemed so happy during this time of his life. I can remember him randomly putting his arms around my waist and picking me up. One day during the summer after Tim's death his friend Kevin randomly picked me up. I filled with emotion because I had not thought about Tim doing that for so many years. At the eighth grade graduation ceremony, Tim gave his speech as salutatorian and also received another award based on character, community service, and leadership. Tim was amazing, and we were so proud. The love I felt for Tim, as well as my entire family, seemed limitless. I can honestly say that was one of the happiest and proudest moments of my life.

# Chapter 17

*Early June 2008*

How to communicate with Peter and David? That became a daily challenge, which I struggled with tremendously. As typical teenage boys, Peter and David rarely wanted to have conversations with me in general, even before the elephant of Tim's death entered the room. How often should I say, "I love you"? We've never been the type of family to verbalize it daily, like each time we say good-bye or good night. On one hand, I now wanted to say, "I love you" every time we parted, but on the other hand it didn't feel natural for me, so I can imagine it would feel a lot less natural for them. I decided not to go overboard, but I did add in the expression of my love more frequently than before.

During the first month or two I found myself trying to be home much more than usual so that I could be available if Pete or David wanted to talk. I put so much effort into trying to be busy in plain view of where they would walk into the house. When I asked if they wanted to talk, about Tim or about anything, they always said no, and they rarely started conversations about him or how they felt, which made me feel sad. I frequently reminded myself of the saying, "You can lead a horse to water, but you can't make it drink." We resorted to what I would consider to be "safe" conversations, such as how school and practice went, grades, schedules, etc. I admit that I was often walking on eggshells, and perhaps they were too.

Andy rarely brought up the subject of Tim either. He did listen and respond, though, as I frequently discussed everything and anything about Tim. As the years since Tim's death have passed, not a whole lot has changed. Discussions about Tim are more natural and comfortable than they used to be. However, I still start most of them and all three men in my household do not, and perhaps never will, discuss their feelings or their sense of loss. While I certainly wish we could engage in those conversations, I accept that we do not and I continue to reach out to my grief counselor and many supportive friends.

During private conversations with Andy I would often elaborate on the reasons I felt guilty about Tim's death and I would also let Andy know the areas for which I held him accountable. Sometimes he agreed, other times he disagreed, but he always heard me out and allowed me to have those feelings. I believe Andy's acceptance of my speaking freely about Tim greatly contributed to our staying together.

I do not believe Tim's death was due to any one specific action or any one specific person. I believe there are hundreds, if not thousands, of factors that contributed to Tim's death, such as genetics, parenting styles, influences from other people of authority (grandparents, teachers, coaches, older friends, babysitters…), each peer relationship, and each romantic relationship. Many people own very small pieces, but I feel that Andy and I own slightly larger pieces. I have come to live with that, and Andy accepts my feelings.

# Part III

# Chapter 18

Tim had never been one to sleep late, nap, or spend much time in his room until the summer before ninth grade. Sometime in early August 2004, I began to observe some changes in him. This was just after Tim graduated from eighth grade, which had been one of the happiest periods in his life. Maybe this was a normal development for a teenage boy? Also, he seemed to be seeing less of his solid group of nine boys. At first when I asked Tim about it, he just said, "Nothing is wrong." I knew this was a very common age for teens to begin experimenting with drinking and drugs, so I asked about that, but received no information. I was glad that preseason for the high school soccer team would be starting on August 15. In addition to working a small part-time job as a server in an assisted-living facility, Tim would soon have practice six mornings a week and would sometimes have double sessions. After my repeatedly asking about his friends, Tim told me that some of them were mocking him for playing soccer because they would be playing high school football, "a real sport."

One night Tim arrived home dirty and disheveled, and he cried in his room. With much persuasion he eventually admitted that one of his friends had fought him. Thankfully, it appeared that three of the nine boys remained close to Tim: Mark, who would be attending the local Catholic high school and playing soccer there; Logan, who would be playing soccer with Tim at MHS; and Tom, who was planning to go out for the MHS cross-country team. However, Tim was moping around in a way that I hadn't seen since maybe the first few weeks after we had moved to Spring Lake Heights, years earlier.

One evening in late August, Tim came home from Mark's house upset. He explained that he had been inside Mark's house with his bike parked outside. When he came out later, he found one of his old T-shirts on the handlebar of his bike. Under closer inspection, he could see that part of it had been burned. Tim had asked his friends, or now maybe not-so-much friends, and he said they had been laughing and wouldn't admit who did it. I was extremely upset, but agreed to stay out of it at this point. I did not know the whole situation, and I am not one to assume that my child's version is the only side of the story. I asked Tim to let me know if anything else occurred, especially anything that might endanger him.

On August 29, 2004, the incoming freshmen and their parents were invited to an orientation session, which would be followed by a dance for the entire freshman class. Spring Lake Heights is one of the seven sending districts to Manasquan High School, and because Tim had played school sports and recreational sports, he did know some of the students from the other schools. There also had been dances for seventh- and eighth-grade students from all of the sending districts. That night Tim absolutely refused to go to the dance, even though all of his Heights friends were going and regardless of how much I encouraged him. This was unlike middle school where he willingly participated in social events. I tried to keep my thoughts positive, such as my being really glad that Tim was enjoying the high school soccer practices. I offered Tim words of encouragement, explaining that he would soon become comfortable with a blend of old and new friends.

To this day I do not know exactly what was going on that summer before Tim entered high school. Although he always had issues with confidence and self-esteem, I never felt he was the same kid after that August. In the early weeks and months following Tim's death, I approached some of the boys who sort of dropped him that summer of 2004. Everyone was very closed-mouthed. One of the other parents tried to get her son to open up and did not succeed either. Approximately two and a half years after Tim's death, I had a meaningful conversation with one of the six boys who had gone out for football. He told me that it wasn't about football vs. soccer at all. In his opinion, the boys had decided that they no longer wanted to follow Tim's lead all the time. They still accepted him as a friend but did not always want to do what Tim chose for the group. Although I do not know for sure, I can speculate that Tim was often the one to suggest what the boys should do that day, such as play basketball, street hockey, video games, etc. He always exhibited tremendous energy, and I suppose he had become used to calling the shots.

I believe something inside Tim changed that summer. Was it related to puberty, relationships, substance use, or some other cause? Sometimes the hardest part for me is accepting that I'll never know the answers to so many questions. Even harder is accepting that Tim may not have known either.

# Chapter 19

As my family unit passed the one-month mark of Tim's death, I began to observe how much I was changing and yet how difficult it seemed to accept each other's changes. I felt that I could not multitask the way I always had, and my kids were not ready to accept that. I received comments such as, "What do you mean you didn't wash my lacrosse socks?" and "I told you I needed new deodorant!" If I tried to explain that stress was taking a toll on me or that I wasn't operating at full capacity, they did not want to hear it. Maybe my children should have been doing more for themselves by this age, but I hadn't asked them to. I hadn't minded handling most of the day-to-day chores as long as the boys did well in school and participated in lots of activities, both organized and informal.

In addition to feeling that I was disappointing Pete and David, I had a hard time accepting my own limitations. I was always proud of my ability to juggle many tasks, and I had to adjust my own expectations. Once again, my counselor, David C., acted as a great sounding board and always helped me—well, more than helped me, he *hounded* me—to believe how well I was actually coping. Andy often just sat in his reclining chair staring at the TV, and I sometimes became angry with that. I remember expressing that I wanted him to take more of an interest in Pete and David; they needed to know how important they still were to him. With help from David C., Andy picked up a new hobby: fishing off the beach. Occasionally David went with him, but he primarily went alone. I found out months later that he was fishing at the spot where we had recently deposited some of Tim's ashes. I felt a sense of relief that Andy was spending time where he would most likely be thinking about Tim, especially because he didn't speak much about him. With time, we all began to settle into our "new normal," as David C. would say. The dynamics in our house never felt exactly like they did when Tim was there, but we were figuring out how to be a family, while each finding our own space again.

I also talked to my sister, Denise, multiple times a day. She had the hardest time putting the railroad scene out of her mind, possibly because she accompanied my father to the railroad the day after Tim died. She did not want to go but my father had insisted, and she did not want him to go alone. Unfortunately, many of Tim's friends had visited the railroad also. Andy and I did not go, but I learned later that the area had not been cleaned up as well as it should have been. Apparently some remains could still be detected that following day. Denise would steadily revisit the scene with me and ask questions we could not answer and I didn't even want to answer. My own recurring stabs varied, though they were not as consistent or physical as Denise's. I would get stuck on one argument I had with Tim or a sarcastic exchange between Tim and Andy or Tim's reaction to being disappointed by a friend. Sometimes one specific memory would haunt me for a few hours, other times for a few days.

One of my daily difficulties was my parents calling to ask if I was alright, how the kids were doing, and worst of all, to administer what I recall as cross-examinations. My parents continued to make statements like, "Maybe Tim really didn't want to go away to college, but you were making him go," or "He was so sensitive and Andy didn't treat him that way," or "How could the doctors not see it coming?" or "Those medications were bad for him," or "That girl who met him at the tracks should be punished!" Although they were just expressing their own grief, I felt they were too stuck on looking for blame. I often felt like I was being cross-examined by a prosecutor. On one occasion, David C. offered to intervene—to call them and explain that they needed to work through their grief with someone who was farther from the crisis, *not with their daughter*, who was grieving even more. At first I said yes, but within a few hours of leaving my appointment with David C., I called him back and reversed my decision because I knew it would hurt them too much. Could it be that some of my family's over-expressiveness and lack of boundaries is due to our 100% Italian descent? It may sound like a stereotype, but I think it may be the truth. I had to deal with them myself and learn to get better at saying things like, "I don't want to talk about this," and "It's too hurtful for me to continue to go over these details again and again."

Occasionally, my parents would anger me enough for me to get ruffled and upset. I recall saying to my father, "Well, what about the genetics he gets from your side of the family's mental health issues? I think genetics play a larger part than environment. Why do I have another child, only thirteen months younger, who is extremely different?!" I tried not to allow them to push my buttons but sometimes I made poor decisions. David C. would always reinforce the concept that we cannot do things right all the time; we all make mistakes and just need to move on from there.

Within a few months, the interrogations slowed down, with the exception of one topic. My mother to this day still repeatedly states, "I pray for Tim every day." I would often reply, "Tim is in heaven with God and he is *safe*. You don't have to pray for him because he is already there. Why don't you pray for the rest of us who have to accept his loss here on earth?" These discussions continued on significantly longer and still resurface occasionally. I personally think this goes back to my question to Father Brian the day after Tim's death: "Can Tim go to heaven even though he committed a mortal sin by taking his own life?" I have learned to let my mother believe as she chooses, most of the time. However, I still have my moments of trying to convince her that if she "misses a day" of praying for Tim, he will not burn in hell. Those are *not* my mother's words, just my interpretation of how she feels and what she has been taught.

# Chapter 20

*2004–2005*

Tim started high school on a Wednesday. That Saturday night, Andy and I realized Tim had been drinking. He came home speaking very loudly and with some cuts and scratches on his body from falling off his bike. When confronted, he eventually said he *found* some beer. Tim was grounded for the following weekend and he said, "This is what kids in high school do." Our response to that was, "Not all kids, and NOT YOU."

In the fall of his freshman year, Tim did very well academically but seemed to gravitate toward a group of juniors. There were a few more instances of drinking, followed by punishment. I was worried about Tim's well-being—his emotions and his physical safety. Maybe this was typical freshman behavior? Did it have everything or nothing to do with the loss of some of his Spring Lake Heights friends?

One day that fall, I did phone the mom of one of the ex-friends from Heights, because he was continually calling Tim's cell phone and harassing him. I explained that my phone call was not to address whether they are friends or not, but to simply put an end to the harassment, which did slow down, or so Tim said.

One nice reprieve for Tim was that at the conclusion of his freshman soccer season, he began his part-time job at Hoffman's Ice Cream, where he remained through high school and made many friends. I have been told by Tim's coworkers that he did some funny things and he was very entertaining. Although this is not nice, I did laugh at a story about a customer who was extremely impolite and demanding. Tim decided to take the wrapper off of a sugar cone, break the bottom of the cone, then put a new wrapper on and smile while handing over the ice cream cone. The staff kept a straight face and watched the customer walk out of the store, knowing that sooner or later he would be wearing the ice cream all over him. I have also been told that Tim and his coworkers competed to find the most ridiculous way to greet customers with names such as bro, man, guy, sir, captain, boss, or even sweetie and doll face for women.

Tim was comfortable at Hoffman's, and many of my friends have shared with me that they will always remember his smile, how polite and friendly he was, and the generous servings they received when he waited on them.

MHS has block scheduling, meaning that the students take half of their subjects during the fall semester and half of their subjects during the spring, similar to college semesters. When the second block began in late January 2005, Tim immediately became friends with a boy he met in science class. This boy seemed to have a lot of freedom for his age, and the drinking incidents increased. Tim had also shown up with red eyes from time to time, and we began to question whether he was using drugs or maybe huffing (inhaling fumes) from aerosol cans. When I phoned the boy's mother to discuss the alcohol use, she remained in complete denial, explaining that her son had a medical condition and that he knew better. Throughout Tim's high school years I found that many parents were either in denial or simply did not want to know about what their kids were up to. I don't honestly know how much drinking goes on in high schools throughout the country, or even the remainder of New Jersey, but high school drinking is fairly prevalent in our area. As spring approached, Tim did agree to go out for the track team, but unfortunately a broken collarbone from snowboarding caused him to start the season late and a broken hand from a fall while running at practice ended the season early, leaving him more free time.

That spring, Tim, who had always been opposed to therapy in the past, asked to go to a therapist because he wanted medication for his ADHD-like symptoms. Tim explained that he was having trouble sitting in science and computers, his two afternoon classes. He stated that he was having difficulty focusing after lunch. After attending a few therapy sessions, he realized that he would not be given meds without ongoing therapy and kind of abandoned the whole idea. I completely supported the therapy, but truthfully, I was not in favor of beginning medication at this point since Tim was still doing well in school. I had serious concerns that the drugs would be used for recreational purposes, or maybe even given to someone else. In retrospect, I believe I made the correct decision *not* to start ADHD meds then. If given the opportunity to back up to Tim's childhood, I might choose to start Tim on ADHD medication back in early elementary school. Perhaps it might have helped with the increased impulsivity and risk-taking behaviors that were now occurring in the early high school years. More questions that will always go unanswered...

# Chapter 21

*Mid June 2008*

Where we wanted donations to be made was another detail from the early days after Tim's death. I did not want to decide right then, but I felt I had to because people wanted to know what they could do. I knew that I wanted something with long-term impact, not just numerous large arrangements of flowers. In order to direct this, the decision had to be made before the obituary hit the newspaper. I originally thought donations should go to the Drug Abuse Resistance Education (D.A.R.E.) program in our town or in southern Monmouth County. Then my friend Mary came to the rescue again and suggested a scholarship fund for Tim's peers at MHS. Mary and I are not "BFFs." We met when our sons began playing traveling soccer together in 1999 and thoroughly enjoyed being MHS soccer moms together and co-hosting pasta parties. Although we don't see or talk often enough, we know we will always be there for each other. David C., my grief counselor, is also a Presbyterian minister. He would chuckle when I referred to Mary as my "religious friend" and say, "I want to be your religious friend too."

We designed the Timothy Schenke Light of Hope Scholarship to reward individuals who are willing to help others in their time of need, the type of people Tim could have reached out to. We decided on peer nomination or self-nomination and received more than thirty applications. The format was very simple, and the submissions were so fulfilling to read. With help from my son Dave, I chose a plaque that now hangs in Manasquan High School with the names of all award recipients to date. Andy and I also designed beautiful certificates to present along with the envelopes containing the scholarship money. On June 9, 2008, Andy and I found the courage to present the award in person to four deserving members of the senior class.

The evening was difficult. Some of the presenters chose to sit up on stage, but Andy and I sat in the audience with a few close friends. When it was our turn to present, I gave a brief description of the scholarship criteria and then Andy and I took turns awarding the winners. I had chosen two or three lines to be read from each of the applications, along with the winners' names. I think the most emotionally challenging moment for me was reading the line from the award criteria, "Although Tim was a scholar and an athlete, we chose to award individuals who help others most—the kind of friends Tim could have turned to had he chosen to do so." Even though I was completely drained, I am so glad Andy and I had the strength to attend and personally distribute the awards.

Just before the ceremony began, one of the National Honor Society members asked if the officers could speak to us afterward. Tim was an executive board member of the Manasquan High School chapter and would have been a presenter that night. The group of four officers and two advisors presented Andy and me with an Academic Letter, awarded to those students who earned a ninety-seven or above out of a possible one hundred points. Tim would have been ranked number four in his class, and only the top five members of the class of 2008 had earned this honor. We also received a long honors tassel, which would be worn exclusively by NHS members at the graduation ceremony. I then completely broke down and sobbed, but it was as much a pleasurable rush of emotions as it was sad. By the time Andy and I got home that evening, we had decided that we would definitely not attend the graduation ceremony. We kind of wanted to see Tim's friends graduate, but it just would have been too painful, and we wouldn't have had a specific purpose there as we had at the awards ceremony.

One other very significant conversation occurred the evening of the awards ceremony. One of the NHS officers, Caitlin, told me how Tim was such a source of strength to her throughout her sister's illness the year before. She spoke briefly, but said I could contact her for more details any time. And of course I did. I contacted Caitlin sometime during the summer, and we continued the discussion. She told me that Tim had first approached her during a gathering at someone's house and had asked her to go outside with him. When he asked how she was handling her sister's condition, Caitlin said, "Fine," but Tim would not accept that. He persisted until she opened up to him and shared her true feelings. Caitlin explained that Tim would check on her every morning in school to see how she was doing and that he would drive her to the hospital to be with her family and wait out in the car because he didn't want to intrude on family time. I had no idea! This side of Tim's personality seemed to come out of left field. I was so glad Caitlin had shared this information. Thinking back, Tim often tried to hide his soft side—both from us and from some of his closest friends. I believe he did not want any praise or thanks because he somehow could not accept that kind of attention.

# Chapter 22

Tim's attempts to *help people* did not always result in positive outcomes. In July 2005, the summer before Tim's sophomore year, he found himself in a little more trouble. I was called by the parent of a girl one year younger who said that Tim supplied her daughter with alcohol. When confronted, Tim admitted that he had a friend who was seventeen years old, looked older, and was served in a liquor store regularly. He explained that he had delivered some beer to this young girl and her friends, but he hadn't stayed. So I asked Tim the obvious questions: "Did you drink? Did you make a profit? Were you trying to get a date with this girl or one of her friends?" After Tim responded "No" to all the questions, I next asked, "Then why?" He said he was just helping them out. His punishment was meted out: We forbade Tim to spend time with the boy from science class and that group of friends, his phone was taken away and his phone number changed, and he was only allowed to see people at our home and have short visits to his childhood friend Tom's house for the next three weeks.

And yet, throughout sophomore year, Tim seemed to really be in his zone, at least superficially. Tim's friend Brian, who had transferred to MHS from the local Catholic high school, was now a member of the soccer team and was spending time with Tim and Tim's good friend Logan. Brian's mom happens to be my "religious friend" Mary. Tim sometimes attended Catholic Youth Organization functions with Brian, which included lots of volunteer work and playing in a basketball league. He had joined the MHS Key Club, a volunteer group that requires community service hours, and he was building up his volunteer hours and beginning leadership projects so that he could apply to the MHS National Honor Society. When Tim decided that he would play only one high school sport, I required that he be highly active in community service, and he did not object. He also earned his best grade point average ever during sophomore year, while taking four honors courses. Even with this course load, Tim did not have to work very hard. He was a natural and only had to put in minimal effort.

Tim's Honors Algebra II teacher, Mrs. Freda, recognized Tim's ability to help others and asked him if he would tutor his peers. He willingly gave up his study period every day to tutor them. He would go to Mrs. Freda's classroom and they would divide up the students who came in for help.

During the middle school years, Tim had developed a great relationship with his basketball coach/math teacher, Mr. Kuriscak. Each summer during high school he worked with Mr. K. at basketball camps, and he was now assisting with the elementary school team.

Despite all the positives, the risky behaviors persisted. Tim had become close friends with some older boys from town, and was spending large amounts of time at his friend Gary's house. Just after Christmas 2005, I found a used marijuana bong, made from a water bottle, in Tim's room. I actually had to show another adult and ask what it was because Andy and I had no idea. Unlike many people from our generation, neither Andy nor I have ever smoked pot or taken any type of illegal drug. I ordered a drug test online and tested Tim's urine, which showed positive for THC, the active chemical in marijuana. Tim was not happy about having his urine tested, but he knew he had no choice. He was punished and missed going out that New Year's Eve. I'm fairly sure this wasn't the first time Tim smoked pot; however, it was the first time we found evidence of it in our home, which warranted punishment and ongoing surveillance.

Throughout the next several months we found evidence of pot from time to time and when we randomly checked, Tim tested positive for THC. I contacted a new therapist. Tim attended a few individual sessions, and we all attended a few sessions together as a family. When I expressed to the therapist how concerned I was about the pot, combined with Tim's attraction to risk and his low self-esteem, he offered us a few options. He explained that Tim had admitted to him during their conversations that he was unwilling to stop smoking weed. Our choices were live with the marijuana use, because many teenagers go through this phase, or send Tim to an intensive outpatient program. When we asked about inpatient treatment, the therapist indicated that not only would insurance deny us, but also that no facility would even consider admitting him based on marijuana use only with no history of outpatient treatment. The IOP would be a few afternoons a week for several hours. I would have to drive Tim, against his will, to each session, approximately forty minutes away. I clearly remember how distressed I was at this point and the strain that was building in our household. Looking back, this was just a preview of the far more intense anxiety and tension that would come later.

Things seemed to be going great for Tim: academics, community service, soccer, etc. But what to do about this new development? Andy and I decided that we would not, could not, send Tim to the IOP. With Andy working full time, how could I physically force Tim there against his will three times a week? We also worried that if Tim went to the IOP, he would be exposed to teenagers who were doing a lot worse things. With Tim's highly impulsive personality and his ongoing attraction to risk, he might get more ideas and make more of the types of friends we did not want him to have. I battled with the following question for a long time: "Is it possible for Tim to be a healthy, happy teen who just happens to be making bad choices?" We decided to forbid Tim from spending time with Gary and Gary's friends. He was extremely angry, and I soon found out that he was sneaking around and lying. At this point, I accepted that I could not control whom Tim was spending time with. I told him I would rather know where he was and I hoped that would put less stress on our relationship.

# Chapter 23

Two to three weeks after Tim died, Peter began discussing tattoos. We repeatedly talked to him about what a permanent decision it was and how he should not rush into it. Pete is not an overly impulsive person. He usually thinks through his decisions after an initial period of overexcitement. Pete asked a friend from school to sketch out his idea for the tattoo, and they worked on it for weeks. The design was incredibly elaborate. It was a cross with Tim's name, birth and death dates, and the word "Heights," surrounded by angel wings in the shape of a heart. By the end of May, Andy and I agreed that we would give written permission for the tattoo, which was necessary because Pete was under eighteen years of age.

I began to think to myself that if Peter could go through with it, then so could I. I had an idea about designing something with Tim's name and a cross as well. When Pete and I went to see the tattoo artist to discuss his design, the timeframe, and the cost, I browsed all the displays of tattoo samples. When I saw a cross with a sunset behind it and a small blue banner for a person's name, I knew that was the one for me. I am impulsive; I can make decisions quickly when I see the right thing. I have often grieved over how Tim could inherit my impulsivity but not my ability to manage my life in spite of it. Tim liked to live in the fast lane: drive fast, jump from the highest tree, take any dare, and sometimes hang around with people who I consider high-risk. As I write this, I realize that while he and I were both impulsive, Tim was always drawn to risk like a magnet, while I am not, and that is a huge difference. As for the tattoos, Pete and I made appointments for June 7, 2008, with two different tattoo artists at the same time. Pete's tattoo took three sessions of two hours each, while my entire tattoo took twenty minutes to complete.

Sometime during the month of May, I began sleeping with one of Tim's "blankies," as I affectionately call them. Beginning at a young age and through maybe late elementary school, Tim slept with several thermal baby blankets. Some were more worn and washed-out than others. I can remember his being embarrassed about the blankies and tucking them away when friends came over. He seemed to eventually replace the comfort of the blankies by sleeping with lots of pillows around his body.

We get our house cleaned every two weeks, and on one occasion, when Tim was a young teen, the cleaners placed the blankies on a shelf in Tim's closet. They never came back out after that. On one of my sleepless nights, I thought about the blankies, got up and went to Tim's closet, and brought one into my room. To this day I still sleep with it under my chin. I have also given one of Tim's blankies to Gary, the friend of Tim's who we first barred him from seeing and who continued to struggle with Tim's death as well as his own issues.

On the morning of June 7, the day Pete and I were scheduled to get our tattoos, I woke up and had a strong feeling that Tim was telling me to rub the blankie along my face. Actually, I almost felt that he had taken my hand and moved it to my face for me. As I rubbed the blankie against my cheek, I began to cry because it felt so much like Tim was there. This was my first experience of really feeling Tim's presence. I have had very few of these encounters. I cherish that moment and also took it as a sign of approval for the tattoos. My tattoo came out absolutely beautifully and I was beaming for days. It was also a great bonding experience for Pete and me.

The members of my immediate family were not the only ones memorializing Tim. Many of the young people had been searching for ways to honor Tim's memory. Only a week after Tim's death, my sons were surprised with a touching gift. Tim's favorite music group was the Red Hot Chili Peppers. Jamie, a friend of Tim's, somehow managed to make contact with a member of the group who sent Jamie an autographed photo. Pete and David continue to treasure it and alternate displaying the signed photo in their bedrooms.

Beautiful displays of affection and warm memories were shared on Tim's Facebook memorial page daily: personally written poems, "miss you and love you" type messages, and quotes and verses from various songs, including "I'll Be Missing You" by P. Diddy. Another friend had designed sweatshirts containing the phrase, "Take me to the place I love," from a Red Hot Chili Peppers song and was having a difficult time keeping up with the demand. A neighbor, her daughter, and another friend designed and ordered memorial stretch bracelets to honor Tim. The bracelets read "Stay Blue and Gold" on one side, and the name "Timmy" framed by two soccer balls on the other side. They were produced in both blue and gold, the Spring Lake Heights town colors. The bracelets were a big hit, and I am touched to see people wearing them even now, years later. Andy, my mother, my mother-in-law, and I continue to wear the bracelet every day. Early on, David wore one on each ankle.

Was I ready to slow down with memorializing Tim? At least one sympathy card had been arriving each day. Even though the personal notes in the cards might have made me sad, I looked forward to getting the mail each day. The first day we did not receive a card occurred about six weeks after Tim's death. I felt disappointed or maybe even afraid or maybe somehow empty. Was the "outsider" grieving now over, and everyone was now just going to move on? I think the real question was, "Do I want to move on?" The answer to that question was, and still is, yes and no. Yes, I wanted to move forward, but no, I didn't want to abandon the grief or forget how sad I was feeling because I never want to forget my son.

On the day of Pete's second tattoo appointment, one week after the first, Andy accompanied him and got his first tattoo: a soccer ball with the number six, Tim's number, and Tim's name. Pete's tattoo is on his chest, mine is on my outer ankle, and Andy's is on his bicep. When Pete decided he wanted his tattoo on his chest, we asked him to consider that a woman might not like that later. Pete had several responses to that, some very humorous and not appropriate for this book, but he somehow proved to us that he would not suffer consequences later.

Yes, it is true, like potato chips, it *is* hard to have only one tattoo. We don't have many, but all three of us have not stopped at one. David would like to get a tattoo in the future too, but he accepted our advice that he was too young and not physically mature enough. His body would grow and that could distort the shape and placement of a tattoo. David already knows that he would like his tattoo to be modeled after a piece of artwork completed by Tim's friend Logan. Tim loved skateboarding and watching other skateboarders at Love Park in Philadelphia. Logan designed a blue and gold figure that read LO on the first line, VE on the second line, and TS on the third line, using the type of script from the "Love" statue at Love Park. I think the tattoo planning activities have been an incredible bonding experience for my now reduced family.

Pete's third and final appointment was scheduled for Friday, June 20, 2008, which was the day after the last day of the school year. Pete did not complete his tattoo until August, though, because of the next crisis—another teenage death that occurred in Spring Lake Heights at 12:08 AM that day.

# Chapter 24

*Mid 2006*

The summer of 2006, when Tim was entering his junior year, we took a great vacation to Cedar Point Amusement Park in Ohio and then to Niagara Falls, Canada. We are a roller-coaster-loving family. For several years Tim and Pete had been tall enough to go on any coaster, but David had still not reached the required fifty-four inches in height. Why Cedar Point? Because it had more roller coasters in the national top ten list than any other amusement park! I had promised that when David grew tall enough, we would make the trip, and in 2006 we finally made good on that promise.

Our first stop was Cedar Point. Because we were spending three days there, it paid to buy season passes. When viewing our photo badges, Tim stated that if he and I had the same hair, we'd look like the same person. Tim was not only my look-alike, but my child who was most similar to me in personality. We were decisive, high-energy people, and we were very efficient when we put our minds to something. On different occasions, such as when we fished or crabbed, sometimes Tim and I became bored and took a walk while Andy, Pete, and David continued to fish. Looking back, at times neither of us would stop to smell the roses. We shared a need to be on the move, to be active, at least through Tim's early teen years.

I also often identified with Tim throughout his sibling rivalry with Peter. I am also the oldest child, and Pete's efforts to "nudge" Tim often reminded me of the way Denise would aggravate me when we were younger. It often seemed that Pete and Denise would enjoy how easily they could upset us. Tim and I were both very serious and not always open to what our siblings considered to be humorous or playful teasing.

Andy and I enjoy visiting lighthouses and although Tim wouldn't openly admit it, he often enjoyed them too. All three of the boys often rolled their eyes as we drove up to the property of yet *another* lighthouse. As a genuine lighthouse lover, I always squeeze as many lighthouses as possible into all of our vacations, so the Cedar Point trip became a combination of thrilling rides, lighthouses on Lake Erie, and touring Niagara Falls. Some lighthouses we just looked at, while others we climbed and toured. I specifically recall Dunkirk Lighthouse in Dunkirk, New York. Our tour guide was an ambitious college student who gave us altogether *too* much information. Pete went back to the car to take a nap, Dave was bored and showing it, but Tim listened to our tour guide, rather tolerantly. Tim loved United States history. It was his second-favorite subject, after math. We always tried to include fun activities along with the history. At Niagara Falls we rode a cable car on a rope across the falls. We also rode—with raincoats on—in an "adventure jet" boat, which took us over level-five rapids!

Upon our return from the roller coaster and lighthouse vacation, it was the start of school soccer season. Tim became a starter on the varsity team and had a fantastic season his junior year. In a key game against Raritan, one of our biggest rivals, Tim scored the game-winning goal in the second overtime and was awarded "Athlete of the Week" in our local weekly newspaper. I believe Tim was very proud of this accomplishment. When interviewed by the newspaper reporter, Tim volunteered information on his academic success and his plans for college. Ironically, I, who had attended nearly every one of my children's sporting events, missed that game because I had to take Peter for an allergy shot and his schedule was tight. I'm glad Andy was there at Tim's big game, even though I can't believe I missed it! See Appendix B to view the newspaper write-up.

At the time of the Raritan game, Tim had been a midfielder. A week or so later, the team sweeper was injured and Tim was asked to move to that position for the remainder of the game. The sweeper is critical because he's the last defender, just in front of the goalie. Tim had such a great game that Coach Levy moved him to that position permanently. All in all, Tim's junior year soccer season was everything we had been waiting for. He had really come into his game.

# Chapter 25

A ndrew, a close friend of Pete's, was just between the ages of Tim and Pete. Because he had a June birthday, he played non-school sports, such as Little League and traveling soccer, with Tim based on age and birthday guidelines. However, he was in Pete's grade at school and they played all school sports together and were part of the same social circle.

On June 19, 2008, Pete went to the MHS graduation ceremony. Not only was it Tim's class, but Pete's girlfriend at that time, Krissy, was also graduating. We cleared Pete's attendance with the school principal because space is extremely limited, each family was only allowed four tickets, and we no longer had a student who was part of the ceremony. Pete also asked if he could bring Andrew as a guest with one of our other tickets. The principal approved. I believe he knew, as I did, that it would be good for Pete to have a friend there for support. Pete and Andrew had been close since we moved to Heights. Pete, Andrew, and several of their other friends went to a party after the ceremony. A few hours later, Andrew said good-bye to his friends and left the party alone. At 12:08 AM he was struck by a train at the same intersection as Tim.

I vividly remember David asking, "Why would Andrew do this? Now we know that Tim was sick with mental illness. Andrew's not, so why would he do this?" I reminded David that Andrew had some serious issues on his plate. Andrew had been under a lot of pressure as a victim in a local, highly visible case of harassment and abuse, and the trial date was drawing near. As stated in an article in the *Star-Ledger* newspaper on August 9, 2008, "Andrew was one of the alleged victims, and his parents and friends say the emotional toll was profound, making him prone to occasional bouts of despair."

Andrew was one of two boys who had been brave enough to agree to testify against a well-known baseball coach at the local Catholic high school he had previously attended. As it turned out, after Andrew died many other boys agreed to testify, and nine more were added to the hearings. Due to the negative series of events that had occurred, and were still occurring, Andrew had chosen to transfer to MHS in the middle of his junior year, approximately six months before he died. I told David, "Unfortunately, Andrew was experiencing a lot of internal turmoil; not the same as Tim, but he was deeply suffering." This seemed to soothe David and to help him to understand that people were not just randomly copying Tim's actions. Although I was already worrying about that myself, I believe I helped David by pointing to something specific.

As the word spread that Andrew was missing and that he had texted a friend, Bryan, stating that he was headed to the tracks, people gathered at the railroad. Meanwhile police officers, along with some family members and friends, searched for Andrew near the tracks and all over Spring Lake and Spring Lake Heights. We were among the first to arrive at the tracks because Pete called us, wanting us to come. However, he was not looking to Andy or me for assistance. We accepted that and observed him from a distance while trying to comfort so many other teens. Peter was outwardly upset and nearly hyperventilating. He was sobbing and repeating, "This can't be happening, not Andrew, not here, not Andrew." Thankfully, Krissy's presence and strength were extremely comforting to him. The MHS staff opened the auditorium, and we were all encouraged to move from the railroad tracks over to the school immediately after we were notified that Andrew had been found and pronounced dead. Somewhere around 4:00 AM we arrived home, and I think I only slept for about two hours.

Later that morning, Andy and I wanted to go to Andrew's house to visit and try to support the family. That first day, I couldn't even talk to Jackie, Andrew's mom. I wanted to try to comfort her and explain to her that I was doing fairly well, but I just did not have it in me yet. I was still too overwhelmed with feelings of sadness, fright, horror, and guilt. Inevitably, I wondered if Andrew would have ever gone through with this had he not been shown the way by Tim. When I expressed this to a few friends, they all replied similarly, "You *cannot* take on any guilt here." Eventually, maybe a month or so later, I did express my guilt to Jackie and she kindly responded, "Please Lisa, don't ever feel that way." The second day after Andrew's death, and many times thereafter, I was able to talk to Jackie one-on-one and offer support. Jackie is a very strong individual, and I think we both greatly benefitted from each other's progress. We both shared a common goal of wanting to reach out to our sons' friends and any teenagers or young adults who were struggling. We also both felt closer to our sons by listening to their friends talk about fun times they had shared. Coincidentally, Jackie had been the person to suggest and arrange for us to meet Father Brian, the priest who led Tim's memorial service.

How could this be happening? While I had previously been more worried about David, now I was becoming more worried about Pete, who now had to suffer another extremely difficult loss. Andrew had been there for Pete and for me. I am so grateful that I had previously expressed to Jackie how helpful Andrew had been, and I had asked Andrew if his mom told him I called her. He said yes and gave me one of his big smiles. Ironically, when we got home from visiting Andrew's family, we found Tim's autopsy report waiting for us in our mailbox. We had been told it would arrive seven to eight weeks after Tim's death, and it did, right on time. I remember thinking that it was probably a good day for the report to come because I was already shocked, numb, and exhausted. This was probably the second worst day of my life. As we read the summary page, there were no surprises. We had already been told, verbally, what drugs had been found in Tim's system: two strains of marijuana and cocaine—exactly what I had already known because I had performed an at-home drug test the morning of his death. The report also stated that Tim died of "blunt trauma" from the impact of being hit by the train. After we finished the summary page, we continued on to the details. Way too many details. At this point we chose to stop reading. I would not recommend reading such horrific specifics to anyone who has lost a loved one to trauma. We put the document down and never went back to it. Is it necessary to know the condition of my son's brain, his eye sockets? Whether one foot was shattered? The report also stated that 104 photos were locked away in the police station. I think this is more than any parent or loved one needs to know.

In addition to the severe mental trauma we faced after Andrew's death, I now became somewhat haunted by the railroad. I thought the train whistle became louder. I started hearing it more often from inside my house and while bike riding along the ocean. Immediately after Tim's death, people asked me if the train whistle was bothering me, and truthfully, I wasn't hearing it any more than I had previously and I couldn't really hear it from inside my house. The ocean is about the same distance from the railroad as my house is, but in the eastern direction, while my house is to the west. Now, after Andrew's death, I started to feel that my bike rides were being intruded upon by the train whistle. It is possible that the whistle had become louder? Investigations into Andrew's death revealed that he may have been trying to get off the tracks as the train neared. I remember hearing or reading that if the train whistle had been louder, it may have alerted him sooner.

The days following Andrew's death were all too familiar. At the memorial service, Andy and I sat with friends, Pete sat with the speakers because he was doing a reading, and David sat with his own friends. My only comfort was that I felt that Tim was up there in the church and auditorium smiling at me.

The following day was the private service and cemetery visit, which we also attended. It was a beautiful day, and after we got home, we all separated and seemed to do what we individually needed to. Sometimes I just know, instinctively, that separation is the best solution. My sons are old enough to rely on friends, rather than us. Andy and I have different ways of seeking solace. I went for a bike ride, Andy went to get an addition to his tattoo that had been done a few weeks earlier, David went to the beach with friends, and Pete went to look at stereo systems with some close friends. Somehow we made it through.

# Chapter 26

Tim's seventeenth birthday was approaching, which meant he would be taking his driving test. When we repeatedly asked him to work on the parallel parking, he refused and practiced very little. Tim was a very skilled driver, and he didn't want to hear that it always pays off to go over each and every detail for the road test. I had also offered to have the driving school take Tim for the test, but he wanted to use his own car, his used black Honda Accord sedan, and the driving school did not allow the use of personal cars.

The test was scheduled for Monday, December 11, because Tim's actual birthday, December 9, was on a Saturday, and the driving test was not offered on weekends. Our family tradition is that the birthday person can choose what he would like for dinner on his real birthday—home-cooked, takeout, or restaurant. That year, Tim did not want to spend his birthday evening with us but rather chose to spend it with his friend Gary. Andy and I were extremely disappointed with that decision, but we tried to accept Tim's separating from us as another sign of his growing up and exerting his independence. When Monday arrived Andy took Tim for the road test, and shortly after he called me with the bad news that Tim had failed the parallel parking because he had hit a cone.

Knowing Tim's personality and his challenges with patience and self-control, failing the parallel parking test did not come as a complete surprise. As expected, he was extremely disappointed and embarrassed. I told him to go back to school, face the questions from his friends, and just get it over with. That evening Tim sat in his room in the dark. While trying to check on him and comfort him as much as he allowed, I also had to deal with a new problem—David's developing appendicitis. The next morning Tim refused to get up for school and I let it go, partially because I needed to get to the hospital with David. Tim later called me at the hospital and apologized for his unreasonable behavior. I'm not sure if he was actually feeling better or if he just wanted to get out of the house, maybe to self-soothe by smoking pot to help overcome his disappointment.

On Christmas morning, Tim asked to go out for a while. As usual we were celebrating the holiday at our house with the three grandparents as guests. When Tim arrived home for Christmas dinner, I could tell he had smoked pot. I spoke to him quietly about it, letting him know how disappointed I was that he could sit at Christmas dinner with the family and be high. Andy was not nearly as upset as I was. He did not approve, but as usual, he would say something like, "He's still getting the grades; he's still involved in sports." I had about had it with those responses. While Tim was still getting the grades and playing soccer, he was losing interest in other hobbies such as shooting baskets, playing street hockey, and skateboarding.

I was extremely quiet for the rest of Christmas Day. In reflection, I was both hurt by and worried about Tim's priorities. Tim's next driving test was scheduled for the next day, December 26, and this time he passed. The following Friday night, December 29, when Tim arrived home, we smelled alcohol on his breath. I just could not believe Tim would drink and drive the very first weekend he had a license. He had to know that we would be looking for it! This behavior seemed to be part of a pattern. Tim would break the rules, accept punishment, and then cross the line again and break another rule or even the same one again. However, this time Tim did not accept the punishment as willingly. The next morning, about thirty minutes after he had walked out of the house saying he would never come back, I phoned the local police, who found him roaming the neighborhood. Officer Gunnell, who knew all of my children from the elementary school D.A.R.E. program, brought Tim home. He said they had a talk, and he informed us that Tim would stay home but would keep his distance from us during his period of being grounded.

Keeping my emotions at bay was quite a challenge. I was so disappointed with Tim choosing not to spend his seventeenth birthday with us, and I was equally distressed about his pot smoking on Christmas morning. The driving would now be another worry. Rather than completely denying Tim a driver's license, Andy and I decided to try to take it one day at a time; to take away the privilege as needed.

# Chapter 27

I often looked into the sky, far into the distance, for Tim that first summer when I was walking, bicycling, or riding in the car. I'm unsure whether I was looking for his face, a symbol, or just some type of connection. Bike riding was also becoming very therapeutic for me. Prior to that summer, when I had the opportunity to choose between sitting on the beach or taking a bike ride on a weekday afternoon, I often sat on the beach. As the boys grew older and I no longer needed to watch them as closely, I had gained a lot more freedom. My part-time work as a personal trainer allowed me to work from the wee hours of the morning until about noon, with a limited amount of work in the late afternoon and evening. I always cleared my schedule after 2:00 PM to attend my sons' sporting events, medical appointments, and everything else, and I loved benefitting from this type of schedule during the summer too.

Now, in the summer of 2008, I felt more restless sitting still and seemed to feel better and think better with the movement of riding. Besides the riding itself, I also like to people-watch in the coastal towns. I live in such a great place, and it's a treat to see the locals and tourists flock to the beach. I like seeing people happy and seeing them enjoy what I love most.

Just before Tim died, I had been reading the book *Medjugorje*, which is about the sightings of the Virgin Mary in Yugoslavia. My friend Mary had given me the book to pass along to Tim just weeks before he died. I had shared and supported Mary's suggestion and left the book out for a while. I pretty much knew Tim wouldn't pick it up and read it, so a week or two later I started reading it myself. One of the topics the book discusses is how some visitors to Medjugorje saw colors in the sky. Not all saw the colors, but it was common. One day in July 2008 I was riding my bike and I saw a burst of color in the sky. For some reason, I felt certain that this patch of color was for me, either from the Virgin Mary or from Tim. I was tempted to pull over and ask someone else if he could see it too, but I opted against it. I decided that it *was* for me, I wanted it all for myself, and I didn't want or need to know about what anyone else saw. I cried a little, continued on, and after about twenty minutes it faded away. Color is a strong, positive motivator for me. Sometimes I feel that looking at certain colors, especially blues and yellows, lifts my spirits. I almost feel that I can internally feel them or even taste them at times. I believe in signs, and I think I remain open to them without inventing them for myself. My sense is that if you are not open to or actively looking for signs, you will miss some truly important moments.

Andy and I had returned to some of our favorite boardwalks that summer. It wasn't unusual for us to go alone because the boys had become disinterested and frequently chose to stay local with friends, as they had during the previous few summers. When we walked on the Ocean City or Seaside Heights boardwalks, I had such mixed emotions. Remembering the great times with all *three* boys at the same time was so precious and yet so painful. Andy said we didn't have to continue to go, but I wanted to, and the visits remain bittersweet.

Throughout the summer months I completed the thank-you cards and began putting some of the items related to Tim's death away—the banners from MHS that I had hung on his bedroom walls; several Heights, MHS, and uniform shirts with signatures of Tim's friends; stacks of sympathy cards; folders containing newspaper articles and internet printouts; and all of the business papers related to the cremation and burial. When I let a few of Tim's close friends choose a T-shirt from his collection, each of them would smell the shirt and comment that it had "his smell." Funny, I never thought Tim had a smell. I am aware of Andy, Pete, and Dave's personal scents, but not Tim's. I suppose that's because it's too close to my own. It may be because he and I are not fans of cologne and we share the same laundry detergent and soap, or just genetics or human nature.

I had also begun looking through more of Tim's things. I inspected his room regularly, I guess looking for a good-bye note or some very specific evidence of why he took his life, although nothing concrete ever surfaced. I often looked through schoolwork I had saved, especially personal pieces Tim had created or written. I think the most meaningful of all was Tim's tenth-grade English journal. It appeared that some days the students were not told what to write about, while other days they were assigned a topic. The assigned topic that caught my attention was to write about the best day of your life. Tim expressed that the best day of his life was his eighth-grade graduation day because his parents were so happy. Tim had graduated as salutatorian and had given a speech. He knew how happy and proud we were that night. It's hard to express how touched I was; how Tim would choose the expression of our happiness as his happiest day. I wanted to hold Tim and tell him how much I loved him and appreciated his love for us. I wanted to thank him, over and over, for such a selfless choice. The journal entry brought me back to the one and only night when Tim admitted his suicidal feelings to me. That evening, Tim told me, "I love you, even though I don't act it." I have such sadness over so much unexpressed love on all of our parts.

That first summer after Tim's death, neither David nor Peter would allow me to share any of my sadness with them. David's sleeping problems seemed to disappear, probably because he wasn't on much of a schedule. It also appeared that he was able to put away his feelings, which allowed him to function normally. I worried just how long these feelings would stay away, and I'd say they remained dormant until late October or early November when he was less busy because soccer season had ended. I remember David telling me to stop crying and threatening to leave the house if I didn't stop. Pete, on the other hand, would sometimes even show aggression. He became defensive and said things like, "You have no idea why Tim died," or "I hate you for nagging me, and so did Tim!" While David seemed unattached and was bluntly telling me to keep away, Pete seemed to be pushing me away with words, which was not out of character for my most outspoken child. I had to remind myself—and

Andy—that Peter needed to express his feelings, as hurtful as they were to me. Even though Andy isn't usually verbally expressive, I do think he feels the hurt that I feel from our children when I get the back talk—because I am often speaking for both of us. He sometimes responds in my defense, and that can be a helpful or harmful thing, depending on the day.

Around mid-August, I once again insisted that Pete and Dave try therapy, this time with someone different who also had been personally recommended. After one mandatory visit each, the boys declined, and I was again told they were functioning well and I was better off not forcing the issue. It is still difficult to discuss my feelings about Tim with Pete and David. I have to walk that fine line between taking advantage of an opportune moment for conversation and saying too much, which results in shutdown. However, having a discussion about anything that involves Tim now is not nearly as stressful as it was that first summer. And even that small change has made a big difference.

One day, while grocery shopping, I heard the song "Both Sides Now" by Judy Collins playing throughout the store. It triggered such strong feelings that I started crying and for several weeks thought about the line, "There's nothing lost but nothing gained in living every day." I felt it was a depressing phrase, and I had a hard time getting it out of my head. Finally, I decided to look up the lyrics because I wasn't sure of them all. To my surprise, the line is actually, "And something's lost but something's gained in living every day." I decided to act on this message and turn the depressing thoughts into uplifting ones. I try to remain open to as many signals as possible, and music is one of my favorite ways they are delivered.

# Chapter 28

*Post-Christmas, December 2006*

My child was on a collision course with disaster. The drinking and driving that very first weekend Tim had his license, which immediately followed the pot smoking on Christmas, completely sent me over the edge. My usual survival tactics of looking for something positive or trying to chalk it up to Tim's maturing were not working. On a few earlier occasions I had briefly thought about sending Tim away, but I had never actively investigated the possibilities. I spent that Saturday looking at alternatives and found a school in Montana that seemed the closest to what I was looking for. But would this drastic step be necessary?

Andy and I probably disagreed more that weekend than we ever had during our marriage. I knew I was considering desperate measures, but I understood my own kid. While many teens were experimenting with drinking and drugs, I somehow knew that Tim's troubles were greater. I strongly believed that his marijuana use was habitual rather than social, and Tim's drinking was often to excess. I knew my impulsive, sensitive, bright child was losing control. In contrast, I knew that Pete, my second child only thirteen months younger than Tim, drank at times and most likely had tried marijuana, but I also knew that Pete was a different kid. He possessed an appropriate level of self-control. He was not losing interest in other activities, and the friends who he was spending the most time with continued to have diverse hobbies and commitments.

The school in Montana was not a military school, nor was it a school for children with mental health problems; it was a place for teenagers who were making poor decisions but had not yet crossed the line into legal troubles or addiction. The setting was a lockdown environment, and psychotherapy was not part of the regular program. Counseling could be added for an additional fee. When Andy realized that I was serious, he began to panic. I did approach Tim who, of course, said he would run away. He also remained firm that he would not stop smoking pot in exchange for my dropping the idea. I did more reading on sending a child away and learned that a skilled security person could be hired to come into our home during the night to basically "capture" Tim and get him on a plane. Although Tim was fully aware of my plans to send him away, he did not know about the *how*, the "capture."

The school wasn't cheap, approximately forty thousand dollars per year. I tried to convince Andy that Tim's college money would be better spent here. Pete and David became aware of the discussions, but this was such a radical idea that I think they just stayed out of the way. I informed my parents, who were also dead set against the idea. I recall my parents saying, "How can you think of sending your child, our grandson, away? He's your son; he needs to be here with us. You can't take him away from us." I could tell that my mother-in-law, who usually tried to remain neutral, was shocked and also seemed unaccepting, although she was quiet.

By now, a late Sunday afternoon and New Year's Eve, I had Tim accepted into the school, and I had tentatively arranged the "capture." I didn't have Andy's buy-in but proceeded anyway. Because Tim was punished and at risk of fleeing, Andy stayed at home for the entire weekend. I kind of went in and out to try to stay sane. I remember riding around in the car replaying the same Barry Manilow song from one of the holiday albums, "It's Just Another New Year's Eve," and crying my eyes out.

At various times, but especially during this crisis, I had felt the urge to flee. I recall saying to Andy, "If we can't agree on child rearing decisions, maybe you should raise Tim, and I should just get out of the picture." I thought I'd have to get one hundred percent out of the picture because I could never handle knowing what was happening and doing nothing about it. I'd have to run away and almost assume a new identity. Then I'd have further thoughts like, "Would Pete and Dave have to choose? How could we separate the brothers?" Eventually, the irrational thoughts would go away and I'd realize that I could never step out of any of my kids' lives.

Maybe an hour before midnight, Andy came up with an ultimatum that stopped me in my tracks. He told me that he would not go out in public or be involved with anything socially with our other two children if I went through with the decision to send Tim away. I believe Andy threatened to withdraw completely based on both anger and embarrassment. My stomach aches as I write these memories. What could stop my actions to help Tim? Only something that would hurt Pete and David.

I backed down just before midnight. At that moment, I suppose I accepted that I had been defeated. It's hard to say which emotion was strongest: anger, because Andy found a way to put an end to my plan; relief, because I was deathly afraid to go through with it; or fear of doing nothing, moving along the same path. Andy, Tim, and I talked and hugged, but Tim remained without emotion. I found that rather unusual. Was it wrong for me to have expected him to act happy? It seemed that perhaps he wasn't happy either way. The one thing I did know was that I'd have to try to find another approach tomorrow, New Year's Day, 2007.

Since Tim's death, I have had numerous conversations with David C. about that decision. In hindsight, I do believe Tim needed mental health treatment, which I was unsure of at the time. The school I had chosen was not centered on mental health. Additionally, in all likelihood, Tim would have escaped. I don't put much past him, and most people would admit that he was a quick thinker and one of the smartest and most agile boys they had ever encountered. Another thought I have addressed repeatedly with David C. was, "What if Tim had ended his life as a result of being sent away?" Had that occurred, I would never have forgiven myself. I don't know if I would still be here today if I felt I was solely to blame. My parents, however, have apologized a few times for not supporting my decision to send Tim away at that time. They later understood why I had become so distraught and, in hindsight, would do anything to alter the final outcome. David C. and I agree that the ultimate tragedy was probably meant to be and that sending Tim away may not have been the right choice. I suppose I will never know for sure. I used to revisit this subject over and over in my own mind, but now I have somehow learned to let it go and to drop the anger I had been carrying toward Andy regarding the choices we made or didn't make for Tim. I believe we had *both* acted out of love, fear, and survival instinct.

# Chapter 29

After deciding to bury Tim's ashes and purchasing a cemetery plot back in early June, we planned a ceremony for August 9. Since we had not done a traditional burial right away, I thought, "Why not wait for the headstone to be completed?" I did have the goal, however, of conducting the ceremony before any of Tim's good friends went away to college. After talking through my plans and feelings extensively with David C., Andy and I decided to divide the ashes and deposit some into the ocean, while leaving most in the urn to be buried. This seemed to be the most comfortable solution for me since I had originally wanted to deposit the ashes into the ocean, and then changed my plans based on input from Pete and Dave.

We had asked Father Brian to lead the prayers at the cemetery. David C., who is also a pastor, led Andy and me in a few prayers the night we deposited the ashes into the ocean, July 31. It was a calm night, warm with light wind, and the tide was going out, which was also advantageous. After our short ceremony I did not feel anything specific; not sadness, not relief, just a kind of stillness. We parted from David C.—he into his car, and Andy and I into ours. We drove around for a while, stopped at a store for a snack, and then headed toward home. As we neared Spring

Lake Heights, I suggested we ride along the beach again and pass the spot where we had placed the ashes. We were riding in Andy's Mustang convertible with the top down. A few blocks before we reached the street something amazing happened. My favorite song of all time, "Someone Saved My Life Tonight" by Elton John, came on the radio. I blasted the music and sang out loud like I always did. But this time I was also crying and joyful. I sincerely believe that Tim gave me that song. I accepted it as a sign that he agreed we had done the right thing that night. It was a powerful time, and I now felt a full, satisfied feeling—no longer the still, empty feeling I had felt at the beach earlier.

On the other hand, I began to dread the upcoming August 9 ceremony. If not for the Elton John song that night, I don't know if I would have had the strength I needed to continue to prepare and get through the following nine days.

The next day, August 1, I decided that I wanted to make a single program sheet for the burial ceremony. The night before, David C. had read a poem called "Miss Me, But Let Me Go." I decided to include this poem and maybe something else along with a short message from us. On Saturday morning, August 2, I took a walk with a friend and had a wonderful, deep discussion. I drove the Mustang convertible that day, and my friend and I walked near the beach. As I got into the car to return home in the convertible with the top down, I heard the song "Come Sail Away" by Styx. I listened and realized I wanted to use the first two verses in the program sheet. I particularly love the second verse which references childhood friends, dreams we had, and missing out on the pot of gold— but, ultimately finding the strength to carry on. Now my plans for the program were complete.

While preparing for the burial in July, Blondie, one of our three dogs, had become very sick. She had an immune deficiency disorder and had always been prone to illness, but her skin lesions were increasing and out of control. She wasn't eating well and had lost a lot of weight. Tim had always been the closest to Blondie. I somehow knew that *if* Blondie were going to die, she would die at least a few days before Tim's planned burial date of August 9. Then I could have her cremated and put her remains into the grave with Tim's urn. While Blondie was so sick, I remembered something Tim had said about her the winter before his death. On a few different occasions Tim had said, "I think Blondie wants to kill herself." When I asked why, he responded, "The way she just sits in her bed, looking at the wall." I responded with something like, "She's a dog, and a moody girl." Little did I realize Tim may have been comparing Blondie's behavior and actions to his own. Blondie did not die before August 9. She continued to do well, having some ups and downs, and died roughly three years later on August 31, 2011. I felt a strong sense of relief, and a connection to Tim, when Blondie's health improved. I felt that I could have survived her death if it had occurred *prior* to August 9 because there would have been a purpose—for Blondie to be with Tim. However, if Blondie died shortly thereafter, I would have been shattered.

The night before the burial I had a breakdown that was unlike any I had ever experienced. I was shaking and crying uncontrollably, nearly losing my breath. Pete and Dave were either out or working and Andy had gone to visit a friend who was recovering from surgery. I knew Andy was only a phone call away, but was relieved that I was alone and could just let the feelings erupt. I think I was able to release the deep-rooted toxins before anyone returned home. I was baffled by my emotions because I have never been one to believe that Tim was in "a specific earthly place" after he died. I believe his spirit is in heaven, and I am not overly concerned with where his human remains reside. Fortunately, the next day I was calmer; I think every ounce of emotion had been spent the night before. The gathering was on a beautiful, sunny day. I had invited only close friends and family, and I allowed Pete and Dave to invite any friends they wanted. Since I had kept the adult population small, the teenagers outnumbered us. There were maybe twenty-five adults and fifty to sixty teenagers altogether. After Father Brian finished the prayers and left the cemetery, the rest of us stayed a while longer. We talked, laughed, and cried, and I felt better knowing that I had provided Tim's, Pete's, and David's friends, as well as our families, with an opportunity to say good-bye. I now knew the burial had been the right decision, and afterward I was exhausted for days.

Although we didn't plan it this way, the gravestone really stands out against the surrounding stones. It is tall and black, while most of the others are short or flat and gray. I encouraged Andy and the boys to work on the design, which turned out beautifully. The top portion contains the name Schenke, a lighthouse beaming its rays, designed after Barnegat Lighthouse in New Jersey, a sunrise over the ocean beaming bright rays of sunshine, and a few clouds in the sky. The lower portion features a Christ figure looking up to the sky. The top and bottom are divided by three lines: the first contains the words "Timothy A.," the second contains Tim's birth and death dates separated by a small soccer ball with the number six on it, and the third contains the phrase, "Heights Forever."

The presence of a grave created a new conflict for me: How often should I go to visit? I still personally felt Tim's presence more in the ocean and in the sky, but now this memorial existed. One of my clients, Ann, who has also become a wonderful friend, lives around the corner from the cemetery. I train Ann at her home twice per week, and I comfortably settled into a habit of stopping by either before or after each session, primarily to see if anything new was placed at the gravesite, to clean up weeds, or to straighten out the various mementos left by friends. That frequency works, and it's still my default today. Many people, mostly anonymously, bring flowers or trinkets of memories to the cemetery. I genuinely appreciate seeing their expressions of love and loss. There are notes, candles, seashells, coins, jewelry, beer-bottle caps, and a Drexel keychain, which I believe was brought by a Middlesex friend who attends Drexel University, and therefore would have become a classmate of Tim's once again. I have added a black rose, a figurine of a young boy, and a few Christmas ornaments that remain year-round. I take home some of the larger decorations brought by others during various holiday seasons and save them for the following year if they are salvageable. I also placed a black rose at the railroad memorial where the "I love you Tim" Hoffman's shirt resides, along with some candles. Tim's favorite color was black, and I found the artificial black roses one day while shopping in my favorite quaint downtown, Point Pleasant. They seemed perfect.

# Chapter 30

Apprehensively, I got through the remainder of Tim's junior year. Tim was grounded on a few occasions and his car taken away yet one more time. The atmosphere in our home was strained and growing in intensity. The constant upset was bringing out the worst in our parenting. Andy would often resort to making statements to Tim such as, "Why don't you just leave if you don't like the rules here?" or "OK, it's your life, so go ahead and throw it away if that's what you want!" which would set off my alarm buttons and cause me to argue with my husband. On a few of my most frustrated occasions I remember saying to Tim, "I can't live like this anymore. Do you want me to leave this house or die? I will do whatever is necessary to save you from making bad decisions." I recall so many of the early parenting books I read stated that rather than telling your child things like "You are bad" or "You are disruptive," a parent should state what the actions are doing to her or him. Looking back, I don't think that was the answer either.

While I was completely preoccupied, Andy often just wanted to continue on as if nothing was wrong. This can take a toll on a married couple, but we made it through and our love is still strong. At times as I look back, I think that Andy was trying to place our marriage as highest priority, ahead of trying to solve Tim's problems, while I was solely invested in saving my child, at any cost *except* the welfare of my other two children.

As Tim entered his final preseason for high school soccer, he was recognized by Coach Levy as one of the leaders. Tim told me that when the coach spoke to the younger players, he was mentioned as one of the players to look to for guidance. Unfortunately, Tim injured his foot in a preseason tournament, which caused him to sit out the first week or two of summer practice. I'm not sure whether it was the boredom of sitting around or some level of self-sabotage, but Tim began exhibiting behaviors that annoyed the coach. Sometimes it was a small thing like wearing a baseball cap on the bus to a scrimmage, which was not permitted, but other times it was the larger issue of verbally harassing the opposing teammates. Tim sometimes shared information about issues like this with me, although he didn't want to share his feelings about them. I remember saying, "Then take off the baseball cap. Just do what is expected of you." I almost wonder if Tim was looking to remove himself from a leadership role. Similarly, I think Tim was relieved to find out that he would be a member of the National Honor Society executive board, rather than hold an individual office, such as president or vice president. Was he stressed by the pressure or the visibility of these leadership positions? Did he feel unworthy?

Throughout Tim's high school years, he grew to dislike the word "potential." On a few occasions when I would go into my speech about accepting the gifts God has given you and working to your potential, he admitted that he did not want the smarts he possessed. When I asked why he chose to spend time with some people who were nowhere near his intellectual or athletic level, he responded, "They understand me. They are my friends, and I belong with them." At the same time, however, Tim did continue to earn excellent grades. I believe he was conflicted. While he seemed to struggle with accepting his natural intelligence, he was also proud of it. Of course, I was happy he continued to achieve. I tried to shrug off Tim's dislike of "potential," thinking that there were many capable teens who had not yet matured enough to realize this advantage.

# Chapter 31

Although Tim often chose not to seek attention while he was alive, his death continued to receive lots of it. A third local boy, Joe, age twenty and a graduate of Manasquan High School, took his own life by stepping in front of a train in late August. We did not know the family personally, and I didn't know many specifics about Joe, but Pete knew his sister. This time the tragedy occurred several blocks down from where Tim died, in Belmar, the next town to the north. It was now becoming a reality that our community was suffering from a contagion, an epidemic of suicide. With each death I continued to feel that maybe if Tim had not gone through with the suicide, the others may not have either. I continued to tell myself that Tim planned only to take care of his own misery, never dreaming that others would do the same thing. I am certain that he would not want others to consider taking their own lives, and I shared that again and again throughout the next several years in numerous settings, including one-on-one and small group conversations, newspaper interviews, and community gatherings. I talk to many teens and young adults from our community one-on-one, often through Facebook. Sometimes it leads to meeting in person, somewhere private. Sometimes we continue to keep in touch, other times it's just a brief relationship. I believe I am helping them, and the satisfaction it brings to me is beyond words; it can never be qualified or quantified.

Similar to how I felt after Andrew's death, I began suffering from yet more physical reactions to the railroad. After Joe's death I thought the railroad gates stayed down longer, both before the train arrived and after it passed. My feelings were, "DAMN THIS! Now I have to hear it more *and* pause there longer, on foot, on my bike, or in my car, each time I encounter a train!" The memories usually pass quickly, but nonetheless, they take me back to the night of Tim's death.

To date, I still have not ridden on a train, not that I usually use the train for transportation. Throughout my life I have only ridden on trains occasionally. I don't think my reluctance is based on the train ride itself; I think I am most afraid of someone jumping out in front of it. I'm afraid I might start imagining that I see people hiding in bushes, waiting to jump out. That fear is not random. It exists because of what I envision when I think about Tim's death. I was told by Justine, a freshman girl with whom Tim had previously had a two-month relationship and continued to talk to and confide in, that Tim ran diagonally across from where the two of them were sitting and ducked into some bushes just before his death. Because she was on the opposite side and farther down from where he jumped out, she did not see what happened, but did hear the sound of the train hitting Tim.

Now that a third train suicide had occurred in less than four months in our small community, more groups were forming and many more outside consultants were brought in. The public as a whole, including school personnel, police departments, and politicians, were learning better methods of helping those who were grieving, especially teenagers and young adults. We as a community were learning that perhaps the previous deaths were glorified more than they should have been and that maybe the boys were being viewed too heroically. In addition to these three young adults, a few other train suicides occurred in Monmouth County in the same year. It's very sad and stressful to be in the middle of such a complex situation. However, Andy and I attended some meetings, often separately as we seemed to prefer different forums, and tried to help as best we could. I was often told that our mere presence at public meetings and forums was a sign of strength and support to the community. And this was a comfort to me.

# Chapter 32

*November 2007*

Andy and I continued to try to boost and support the positives in Tim's life—the academics and all related activities, the fun of simple outdoor play or active video games, and Tim's physical health. Tim had been driving for almost a year at this point, and we had been paying for his car insurance. There was a catch here, but I think it was a fairly easy one, and Tim had been cooperating. Because I had become concerned that Tim wasn't taking care of himself physically and mentally, I required that Tim work out the equivalent of four half-hour sessions per week in order for us to pay for his insurance. This could be any type of exercise, and it could be done in half-hour increments or two hours all at one time. I explained how I strongly believed that physical activity helps keep a person both physically and emotionally healthy. I also tried to clarify that this was not meant as a form of punishment, but rather as an opportunity to easily earn the car insurance payment.

During school soccer season we never even had to discuss my requirement because the hours were far exceeded. Since Tim had stopped playing club/traveling soccer after sophomore year and he was only playing one school sport now, he had to make the effort at certain times of the year. Beginning in November 2007, at the conclusion of his senior soccer season, Tim decided that he would rather pay the insurance than work out for two hours per week. I was very unhappy with this decision, not only because I wanted Tim to maintain healthy habits, but also because of the trend I was seeing of Tim giving up the hobbies he had always thought were fun. It was painful to accept Tim's money. I did reinforce the fact that he could reverse his decision at any time. However, once Tim made up his mind, he rarely changed it. I suppose I was trying to force him to take care of himself, and then in part taking his money so he would not spend it on alcohol or pot.

One positive memory I have from this period in Tim's life was watching him enjoy the game *Rock Band* with his friend Kevin and his brother David. They all took turns playing the guitar and the drums, but only David and Kevin did the singing. I suspect that was another area where Tim did not want to be the center of attention. I remember feeling happy to see Tim enjoying himself and spending time with David again. They had always been close, but the changes in Tim that had happened gradually through his high school years had distanced them somewhat.

Tim and Pete's relationship continued to be volatile. On one occasion that fall they had an actual physical altercation, for the first and only time in their lives. Pete's punch knocked Tim's two front teeth into his gums, requiring Tim to undergo two root canals and wear a corrective retainer. Andy and I had always known this day would come. Throughout the years, Pete would agitate Tim, and then Tim would respond physically. Or Tim would say something to Pete, and so on, and so on. Normally, one of them would calm down on their own, or one of us parents would intervene. But not this time. By now Pete was significantly larger than Tim, and we knew that one of these days Pete was going to react without realizing his own strength. We had warned the two of them, but our words had fallen upon deaf ears. Thankfully this was a one-time incident, and afterward they seemed to make up, or maybe just dissociate themselves even more.

Andy and I continued to worry not about the physical damage, but about the blow to Tim's self-esteem. When I asked Tim how he was doing the next day, he did admit that Justine, at that point his girlfriend of about a month, was getting her braces off that day, and he said, "Everything happens to me." I tried to reassure him that he would feel and look better very soon. Of course, word of "the fight" spread quickly. Tim returned to school wearing sweatpants and a flannel shirt, uncharacteristically large, loose clothing for him. I suspect he was hiding.

When Tim arrived home from school he asked me, "Who is Apollo Creed?" I explained, "He was the losing fighter in the first Rocky movie," and asked, "Why?" Tim replied, "Mr. Green called me Apollo Creed." I knew that Mr. Green taught both Tim and Pete that semester for different subjects, so I immediately ran up to Pete's room and asked if Mr. Green had said anything to him today about the Rocky movie. Pete responded, "Yeah, he called me Rocky." I asked, "In front of the whole class?" and Pete replied, "Yes."

I was livid. I said to both boys, "I want no more talk of any of this and if it comes up again, you should tell the teacher to end the conversation." I told Tim how sorry I was and that he should not have to accept that type of harassment. At first, I agreed to "let it ride" as requested by Tim. The following day I entered the high school to drop off a note for Tim's one-day absence, due to the dental emergency, and found him sitting in the vice principal's office. I was surprised because this was the first time ever that Tim had been sent to the vice principal's office. When I asked, "What are you doing here?" Tim responded, "I was sent here because I talked out in study hall." When I pressed for more, Tim added, "I cursed." At that moment I turned, entered the vice principal's office, and described what had occurred with Mr. Green the day before. I explained how I feel my son should not have been subjected to such harassment and how I believed it had contributed to Tim's acting out. Tim's punishment was reduced from a one-day suspension to a Saturday detention, but that was hardly the point of my conversation with the administrator. The damage had already been done…

# Chapter 33

*Fall 2008*

I knew exactly what I wanted for a second tattoo and by late summer I had already started formulating my plans. Getting a tattoo is a permanent decision, not to be taken lightly. Because I loved having Tim's name imprinted on my body, I just knew I wanted to have Pete and David's names too. While I'm at it, I decided, why not include Andy's and my name too. I felt that my desire to include Andy's name was affirmation that we would stay together; not that we were ever considering separating, but I had read so many terrifying statistics about how seventy-five percent of marriages end following the death of a child.

I am very fond of peace signs and had seen an image of a tie-dye peace sign and really liked it. I am pleased to say that I came up with my own design which had Tim's name in the middle of the peace sign surrounded by "Andy, Lisa, Pete, and Dave" in the outer circle. Andy and the boys knew about my idea but I did not tell them that I had made up my mind and scheduled an appointment one day in late September. Surprising them was a lot of fun. Of course, Pete's first words were, "If you can have more than one tattoo, then so can I." My response was, "We'll see," and that did hold him off, but only until the following summer.

After Tim's senior soccer season the previous fall, I did not expect to be attending Manasquan High School varsity soccer games for at least another year or two. At this time David was only a freshman and Pete's primary sport was spring lacrosse. Pete had played football freshman and sophomore years, but did not play a fall sport his junior year due to multiple injuries. As a result of Tim's death, Pete's now deceased friend Andrew had convinced him to try out for soccer goalie. Pete had played goalie for years in traveling soccer, but had been away from the sport for a while. Andrew told Pete that he hoped to play the position of sweeper, right in front of the goalie, and he would protect Pete at any cost; they would have each other's backs. Andrew suggested that Pete could play in honor of Tim; he could dedicate his season to Tim. Pete agreed, they played a few summer league games together in early June, and then Andrew died on June 20. That summer I did not pressure Pete about this topic. He had to decide whether he could bear playing without Andrew and try out for goalie in honor of both Tim and Andrew. Pete succeeded in tryouts and had a great season. As a freshman, David played on both the freshman and the junior varsity teams, which is not uncommon for freshmen players with a lot of experience. Tim had played on both teams as a freshman too. David scored his first junior varsity goal in the first game of the season, and I was ecstatic. It seemed so unreal now watching my other two sons play high school soccer at the same time, something I never expected but happily accepted and enjoyed to the fullest.

# Chapter 34

Tim would have happily applied to only one college or university, but I did not allow that for two reasons. Even though Tim was a shoo-in for Drexel—his first choice—there was always that small chance he would not get accepted. Also, the cost of Drexel was well into the forty thousand dollar range per year, and we did not want to carry that much debt, or have Tim carry that much debt in student loans. We knew Drexel had a large endowment, and based on Tim's GPA and class rank he would most likely be offered a generous merit scholarship. Against his will, Tim did apply to three schools, was accepted into all three, and was offered merit money from each of them.

Most colleges require an essay or a personal statement as part of the application. Again displaying his stubborn nature, Tim absolutely refused to write the essay during the summer even though I continued to ask him to do so because he had more time than he would in the fall. As I have said before, there were times Tim could not be persuaded or bribed. As it turned out, Tim's English teacher that fall had each student work on his essay as a class assignment. When Tim shared his draft with me, I truly could not believe what he wrote. The subject was *me*—his mother—and my positive influence on him. I was floored. See Appendix C to read the essay.

I am also embarrassed and sad to admit that, while I told Tim I was flattered, I did not think it contained enough substance. Having read so much about college essay writing, I felt that too many students wrote about the positive influence a parent or grandparent has had on them, and I knew that if Tim chose to use this common topic he should really have a heavy hitter. Maybe this is another area of my personality that rubbed off on Tim: a lack of confidence that I had done anything really worthwhile. Although I felt bad about my suggestion to change the essay, both then and now, I still don't know if I actually offended Tim. He did not seem all that emotionally invested in the essay; he treated it more like a task he had to get done. I suppose this approach matched his personality—unwilling to reveal his inner self and hesitant to bring any attention to himself or his feelings. Tim stated, "Colleges should admit students based on grades and activities, not on a stupid essay." In the end, he used a different topic. We jointly decided he would write about how he had been moved to a new position in soccer, the sweeper, and how much he ended up valuing and enjoying it.

Tim's acceptance to Drexel arrived sometime in November. We were ecstatic, but, half-seriously, I told him not to put the Drexel sticker on his car until we found out about scholarship money. On December 18, 2007, Tim received a letter offering him enough scholarship money to bring the cost down to the middle-twenty thousand dollar range, which was fantastic.

When Tim opened the letter, he didn't act excited. I told him he could now put the Drexel sticker on his car and asked why didn't seem happy. He responded by saying, "I will be happy about it tomorrow."

Tim stayed in his room most of that evening, didn't eat dinner, and didn't want to talk about why. The next afternoon he explained that his girlfriend of about two months, Justine, had broken up with him. I had not at that point met her, as Tim had previously told us that we couldn't meet her and that her parents didn't know about them because of the age difference. I don't truthfully know if that was the real reason, because she later told me that she had asked to come over.

During the middle-school years Tim had many girlfriends. However, until Justine, he had seemed to avoid relationships during high school. I know he dated here and there, but he would never refer to "a girlfriend," at least not to us. Tim also avoided most formal social events such as homecoming dances and the junior prom, though he did agree to go to his sophomore semiformal when he was asked to go by a senior. Kathy, a coworker at Hoffman's Ice Cream, who was a beautiful girl and had been named the homecoming queen of her high school, asked Tim to take her to Manasquan's homecoming dance. Although they were good friends, Tim refused and told me that he "just doesn't go to those kinds of things." I remember thinking and expressing to Tim that he was absolutely nuts not to take Kathy.

After the first few rough days, Tim seemed to be handling the breakup better. On New Year's Eve I mentioned to Andy that this was the first New Year's in three years that Tim was not in hot water with us and was out with friends. I didn't know if this was a good thing or if I should be concerned.

We later learned that Tim had started the new year, 2008, sitting alone in his car.

# Chapter 35

*Fall 2008*

Does everything happen for a reason? I generally believe that it does. However, I continued to deeply struggle with one specific detail surrounding Tim's death. I mentioned earlier that I was reading the book *Medjugorje* at the time Tim died. For the first and only time in Tim's life, he did not come home the night before his death—the night of April 25, 2008. At that point, Tim's curfew was 1:00 AM. As 1:15 approached I began calling his cell phone. Tim finally answered and told me that he was not coming home. I responded by explaining that he was not allowed to stay out all night. Based on prior discussions, our house rule had become the following: if you are over the age of eighteen and don't come home, you will find the door locked in the morning. I also made it clear that I would be disconnecting his cell phone because having a family cell phone is a privilege given to those who act like part of the family. Tim ignored the threats and did not show up. When I finally went to bed at about 2:30 AM, I remembered something that had been reinforced over and over throughout *Medjugorje*, the concept of "giving it to God." Somehow I finally fell asleep after repeating "give it to God" several times.

The next morning I did allow Tim to come home, thank goodness. But there were consequences. This was new territory; we had never actually reached the point of whether to follow through on such a serious, life-changing threat. When Tim called at 7:30 AM asking if he could come home, I made an on-the-spot decision; I told him that he could come home and that he was grounded until his next therapy appointment. I cannot imagine how I would live with myself had I told him he was not allowed back into our house.

For months now, throughout the summer and fall, I had been struggling with that "give it to God" incident on April 25. I told myself that I would *never* say it again. I gave it to God for the first time in my life and look what happened—my son died. I brought this up many times during my sessions with David C. He would explain that he did not have an answer for me. Yes, it was difficult to live with, but God is not punitive. David C. knew, through so many conversations, that I was not mad at God, I just couldn't understand this and I wished I had never uttered that statement.

Sometime during the fall of 2008, David C. expressed something different during one of our deep conversations. He explained that maybe it was already determined that Tim was going to die and God was bringing me to a place that I could accept it. Maybe my stating "give it to God" that night meant that I was ready to accept the outcome. I will never know, but I seem to be able to live with that explanation. I am a very determined and persistent individual and, for the most part, when I want something, I can make it happen. The single most difficult thing in my life for me to accept is that I could not save my son's life.

I sometimes think that Tim had barely bottomed out. He had not been in any legal trouble, he was still living with us and attending high school daily, and he had not lost interest in his schoolwork. He was not *physically* addicted to drugs because marijuana is supposedly not addictive. Tim was always impulsive and intolerant of waiting for things. Could these traits have led him to take his own life before he had reached what would be most people's bottom? I wonder if he could not bear the thought of waiting to feel better.

In a counseling session during the time I was writing this book, I was sharing with David C. how Tim would inevitably strike out when he was at the plate with two strikes. I stated, "I guess he wanted to get it over with since he felt he was going down anyway." David C. had a visible reaction and after a few moments of silence said this insight had moved him in a powerful way and perhaps was a window into Tim's feelings and decision to take his own life.

I tell myself that Tim was not destined to have a good life or God would not have allowed this to happen. I am not saying this is the right way to think, but it is my way of coping. Lots of friends try to tell me not to feel this way; that Tim would have accomplished great things. I will never truly know. I want to clarify here that my feelings are definitely *not* meant to promote suicide as an option; merely that everything happens for a reason. I sometimes pray for God's help and I don't always ask for a specific outcome. When I do pray, I am often asking God for help in accepting what is meant to be. Although I don't actually believe that I *caused* Tim's death with my words, I will *never* say the phrase "give it to God" again.

Months after Tim's death, people continued to reach out to me. I think sometimes it was to help others meet their own needs, sometimes because they wanted to share with me, and sometimes both. Numerous students have told me how much Tim helped them with math, and others with chemistry, history, and other subjects. This help was often just in his free time, not through his official tutoring volunteer work. So many friends have let me know what a reliable and trustworthy friend Tim was.

One mom, whose daughter was a friend of Tim's, contacted me to let me know how Tim had helped her daughter. Tim recognized that her daughter felt that she did not fit in. He had shared his similar feelings and offered support. Mark, Tim's best friend that first summer we moved to Spring Lake Heights and an ongoing friend, told me how he wished he and Tim had gone to the same high school. He felt that if they had both gone to the public high school, or both gone to the Catholic high school, Tim would still be here. Kevin, another good friend of Tim's, admitted to me that he felt somewhat responsible for Tim's death. He explained that Tim had told him that he felt like he was crazy. Kevin responded to Tim that he couldn't possibly be crazy because he was so smart. He felt that he kind of "shut Tim up" and never gave him the chance to continue to share his feelings. Kevin had wanted to talk to me about it and carried that guilt around for nearly six months. I explained to Mark and Kevin, separately of course, how I deal with my guilt and how I am able to acknowledge that I am not solely responsible. I don't like to minimize each puzzle piece, or the importance it has to the other individuals involved. I just try to convince myself, and others, that changing one puzzle piece would not change the big picture. Yes, each piece is important, and yes, we feel that we would do anything to change that piece, but the final outcome would most likely be the same. A whole lot of pieces would have had to be different in order for Tim to have chosen to live.

Just how much of Tim's death is my fault? I will always cherish the day I received direct feedback from one of the two most important people I needed to hear from. One day, while David and I were riding in my car, we somehow stumbled onto the topic of how I sometimes feel responsible for Tim's death. David responded, "Of course it's not your fault, Mom." Hearing those words gave me such a feeling of relief. I always wondered how much Pete and Dave blamed me. I wished I could capture that moment and savor it.

# Chapter 36

Pete came downstairs and told us that Tim's ex-girlfriend, Justine, had called him informing him that Tim wanted to kill himself. After a moment or two of confusion, Andy headed out to catch Tim before his shift at Hoffman's Ice Cream was due to be over at 8:00 PM that Wednesday evening, January 2. When Andy got there, Tim had already left, and we began to panic when he didn't answer his phone. However, he came home about fifteen minutes later and fully denied feeling suicidal. Tim wouldn't offer any information, and Pete claimed he did not have any specifics either.

I wasn't sure what to believe, but knew with certainty that I would not ignore the information. I looked up therapists in our insurance plan and began leaving messages explaining my situation. At 10:15 PM that night a therapist called me back and agreed to see Tim early the next morning. Although Tim still denied the accusation, we forced him to go. After he spoke privately to the therapist, I was asked to join them. The therapist said that he did not feel Tim was a threat to himself, and we scheduled an appointment for the following week. As soon as we arrived home, Tim left for school, and I asked him to call or text me if he was having any bad feelings.

Tim was scheduled for a dental appointment at 4:00 PM that day, January 3. When he and I got into the car to leave, Tim informed me that he had not eaten all day because he was upset. At this point he admitted he was starving, and we stopped at McDonald's. He would not elaborate and went into the dental visit. On the way home Tim opened up to me, explaining that he was upset because he found out Pete had spent part of New Year's Eve with Justine. Rather than being angry with Pete or Justine, he confessed that he wanted to kill himself. I wish I could remember Tim's exact words, or even something close, but I can't. I responded, "Oh my God!" then I believe I went into a rant about how Tim's feelings were not *only* about the girl, that his feelings were due to multiple issues, including his lack of coping skills and his frequent use of marijuana and alcohol. Then I realized I had to try to keep my cool, keep him talking, and keep driving. I next thought to myself, "Damn you, Peter!"

I was somehow able to calm down, and I reminded Tim that he had previously spent an evening with a girl whom Peter was seeing last spring. I expressed that while I don't approve of brothers and friends treating each other this way, it sometimes happens.

I guess once Tim began to open up, he started to just spill. Tim then said, "I've taken other drugs, not just pot. I took painkillers, but not very often." When I asked him what kind and how often, Tim responded, "Roxys," and some other word I can't remember, and "Less than twenty times altogether, during the whole four years of high school." I asked what a roxy was, and he said, "Oxycontin. You didn't catch it on the random drug tests because it wasn't regular." I later learned that opiates, this category of drugs, do not stay in the system more than a few days. If I remember correctly, I just kept telling Tim that we could work on his troubles; his life was worth it and he would feel happy again.

I could not believe what I was hearing and trying to process, so I forced myself to calm down. When we arrived home, Andy was not there. I think he was coaching David's recreational basketball team practice and was due home shortly. I couldn't decide whether to call the police, wait for Andy to get home, or what other action to take. As Tim and I sat in the family room, I heard him say to Gordon, our youngest dog, "I'm sorry I won't get to see you grow up." He then said to me, "I love you, even though I don't act like it." I told him that I loved him more than anything. My heart was breaking, and I felt paralyzed.

Maybe a minute or so later, Tim said, "I'm going to kill myself tomorrow." As I picked up the phone, Tim said to me, "Don't call Dad or the police or I will run away." I sat for a few minutes, which felt like hours, waiting for Andy to arrive. I suppose I had rationalized that Andy would be strong enough to restrain him if he tried to run out of the house while I placed the call. Things get a bit fuzzy from this point on, but soon thereafter I believe I asked him how he planned to kill himself and he responded, "I am going to drive my car into the middle barrier on Route 70 in Brick." Brick is a nearby town that is about fifteen minutes away, and Route 70 is a major, high-speed, four-lane artery that runs along the Jersey Shore.

As Andy entered the house shortly thereafter, I walked into the kitchen and quietly told him that it was an emergency and he should watch Tim while I called the police. As I began explaining the situation to a police officer over the phone, Tim ran for the door. I vividly remember Andy holding him down on the ground, and my yelling to Pete to come downstairs and block the door. Tim was fighting so hard that the police officer had to handcuff him upon his arrival. They brought him to the local hospital for psychiatric evaluation, and I followed in my car. Andy arrived a short while later, after he had confirmed that Pete and Dave would be OK together at home.

The next day, Tim was transferred by ambulance to a mental health facility and I followed, once again in my own car. When we spoke to the admitting psychiatrist there, Tim had a completely different attitude, stating that he was fine and wanted to go home. I recall that doctor saying, "This doesn't sound like the patient the hospital described to me last night." Tim answered each question briefly and asked when he could sign a forty-eight-hour release paper. I had no idea what he was talking about. When we were alone, Tim told me that the EMTs in the ambulance had informed him that if he was over eighteen years old, he did not have to stay. He could ask to be observed for forty-eight hours and then be released. I could not believe the audacity of the EMTs. What right did these men have to plant ideas for release in my son's head? I should have reported the ambulance crew's behavior to the hospital administration, but I guess other priorities got in the way.

Tim had turned eighteen years old on December 9, 2007, less than one month prior to this incident. I still cannot believe that he was treated as an adult. How can an eighteen-year-old, who is still in high school and considered too young to drink legally, be making life-altering decisions about his health? Before I left that day, Tim also stated that he would never tell me if he felt suicidal again. And he never did.

Tim's stay was not only brief, but was over a weekend. He was not admitted until Friday afternoon, signed his "forty-eight-hour sheet," whatever that was, and was "observed" by the weekend staff. I asked as many questions as possible and found that there were no individual appointments and no caseworkers present on weekends. Tim did attend a daily group session, and nurses were present, but he would not be assigned a caseworker who would be in charge of his treatment during his stay until Monday. Andy and I visited both weekend days. David wanted to come, even though we told him that he wouldn't be allowed to go in because visitors had to be over eighteen years old. He came with us on Sunday and waved to Tim through a glass window. By Sunday, I guess Tim was thoroughly disgusted with the mental health hospital. He could not believe that every patient's shoelaces, as well as any drawstrings from their sweatpants, were taken away as a safety precaution. He also felt that so many of the patients were "crazy." His roommate "heard voices all the time," barely spoke a word, and never left the room. Tim had been allowed to go to the gym and shoot baskets during open gym time and complained that there was no one competitive to even shoot around with. He angrily said, "If you don't get me out of here right now, then go home. I don't want to talk to you or see you." When Tim walked back to his room, we picked up David in the waiting room and headed home.

Andy and I had very different feelings throughout that weekend. While Andy agreed that the hospital stay was necessary, he continued to feel uneasy and just wanted Tim to be home. On the contrary, I was relieved that he was in a lockdown, being kept safe from himself—or so I hoped. I realized our behaviors and feelings mimicked the scene from just over one year before when I wanted to send Tim away after his drinking and driving incident on the first weekend he had his driver's license.

Tim was released that Tuesday because, according to the hospital staff, he had proven that he was not a threat to himself or others. I'm pretty sure that the only reason he was retained until Tuesday was because I couldn't reach the proper caseworker until late in the day on Monday. When we spoke she immediately set up his family therapy meeting, which was required before his release Tuesday morning. At the meeting, which consisted of Tim, Andy, me, the caseworker, and a nurse, I asked, "How can you know he is not suicidal?" and was told that the professionals don't know long-term, but suicidal feelings come in waves, and for Tim the feelings had passed. When I asked, "Well, aren't they likely to come again?" I was informed that they cannot keep a patient in the hospital long-term; they are only evaluating for a period of about the next three to five days. This was lunacy! I could not believe what I was hearing. I seemed to have no recourse. I suppose this is how they covered themselves in terms of liability. We had to sign a form agreeing that we would seek outpatient therapy as part of the discharge process.

Against Tim's wishes, we insisted on outpatient therapy with a psychologist for depression and possible bipolar disorder and regular visits with a psychiatrist to monitor the meds he had begun taking. Tim was diagnosed as possibly bipolar based on two pieces of information: One was a possible family history of bipolar disorder on my father's side of the family, and the other was some new research indicating that bipolar disorder in children could be expressed through ADHD-like symptoms. At this point we supported starting Tim on antidepressants, even though we were aware that they may cause suicidal thoughts in teenagers. Tim was already having suicidal thoughts, though, so why not try them. Prior to this incident, all previous therapists had told us that Tim was not depressed, but rather that he was manipulative. I had never believed this to begin with, and I was finally getting confirmation of what I really thought was the problem.

A few days after Tim got home, he told Andy that he had left early from the New Year's Eve party he had attended. Tim mentioned that he just had been riding round in the car alone as the clock struck midnight. I brought it up with him a little later and asked why he left the party and his friends. He said, "I just didn't want to be there." I responded, "I wish you would have come home and spent the start of the new year with us. We would have been happy to have you with us, and we're always here for you." Tim did not verbally respond, and even his facial expression was impassive.

I now celebrate January 3 each and every year because as terrifying as it was, it was also one of the best days in my life. It was the only day that Tim confided in me and told me the truth about how he was really feeling. How I wish he felt he could have relied on me more often.

# Chapter 37

"Do we decorate or skip it?"

"How am I going to celebrate Christmas?"

"How will I be able to deal with all the memory-filled Christmas tree ornaments?"

Outdoor Christmas decorating has always been a very big event at our house. Ever since Andy and I first bought a house, in 1985, we have enjoyed decorating, and things seemed to grow exponentially after we added a porch to our Spring Lake Heights home in the year 2000. We have even won the town's decorating contest several times!

During the latter part of the summer of 2008, just a few months after Tim's death, I started thinking, "What are we going to do about the decorations? How am I going to get through this?" One day that August the answer came to me. We have three large windows on the second floor over the porch, which we generally decorate with ropes of lighted, draped garlands. Rather than randomly draping the lighted garland, I decided we would spell out TIM, with one letter in each window.

We usually started decorating outside in early November because I liked to be finished in time to light up the house on Thanksgiving night.

After my revelation, I couldn't wait to begin the decorating. We typically started with the second floor and worked our way down. So one Saturday afternoon in early November 2008, we worked out the details, assembled the materials, and put up the TIM lighted garland. Just after finishing that task, David asked me to give him a ride to someone's house. As I turned on the car, my favorite song, Elton John's "Someone Saved My Life Tonight," began playing. I was elated. Another sign of approval from Tim!

Each November the students at MHS elect a homecoming king and queen from the senior class and a male and female member of the court from each grade level. Both Pete and David were nominated for their grade levels, and each won the election. I don't think I've ever had such mixed feelings about something in my entire life. I was genuinely happy for Pete being chosen as homecoming king and for David to be the freshman in the court, but my insides were aching because of the upcoming Thanksgiving holiday, coupled with the warmth and meaning of the Manasquan traditions. Thinking about Pete and Dave in the limelight the very first year that Tim was not here seemed overwhelming. I put on a happy face, but I could feel myself sinking. I did find the strength to attend the festivities, which included a parade on Thanksgiving eve and a football game the next day.

I regularly host Thanksgiving dinner and was planning to do so this year too. Part of our tradition is that my mother-in-law is always the person to say grace. At first I asked her if she could keep it light and not mention anything about Tim. As Thanksgiving Day was approaching, I then asked her if she wouldn't say grace at all, deciding to serve the meal buffet style. I did not think I could survive those moments of everyone sitting at the table waiting for the go-ahead to start eating, with or without grace. Tim's absence would be just too excruciating.

I somehow managed to get through the homecoming festivities and the Thanksgiving holiday, but barely. I was emotionally and physically exhausted, cried at the drop of a hat, and felt sluggish overall, which I think was caused by depression. Additionally, Tim's nineteenth birthday would be coming up on December 9 and that was weighing heavily on my mind. The following week, after continuing to cry more than ever, I decided it was time to try some meds and quickly made a doctor's appointment.

Because of suffering from an eating disorder earlier in my life, I had tried medications for anxiety or depression, but I had never stuck with them. My symptoms had been tolerable, and I always felt that the side effects outweighed any benefit. Either that or I didn't even stay on the medication long enough to assess whether there *was* any benefit. However, this time I think I hit it right. The medication and dosage did not give me any negative side effects, I did feel somewhat better, and I am still on this medicine today.

About one week prior to Tim's birthday, I asked Andy, Pete, and David individually what they wanted to do to acknowledge or celebrate the day. Not surprising to me at all, each of them replied, "Nothing," so I figured we would just play it by ear that night. Then, at 9:00 PM the night before Tim's birthday, David seemed very upset and asked if we could do something special the next day. I had to think hard and fast. I told David we would take a half-day and he could ask a friend or two if they wanted to go to ESPN Zone in New York. When he did, each of them was busy with a practice, a game or something else, and I decided against calling the parents to further explain and ask them to make last-minute alterations. Pete had just returned to school after a complicated recovery from having his tonsils removed, and Andy had an important meeting to attend at work, which we agreed he would not skip out on at the last minute.

Since it would be just the two of us, David and I set up a plan that I would pick him up from school at noon to go to a mall or a movie or something. When I got up the next morning, I went to Tim's memorial Facebook page to see what birthday entries and comments had been made. I noticed that Tim's friend Logan was the first person to write a happy birthday note at the stroke of midnight on December 9, 2008, and I knew Logan was still having a difficult time dealing with Tim's death. While I was at one of my jobs that morning, I had a brainstorm: I decided to call Logan and ask about his schedule for the day. If he was free that afternoon, and he was, Dave and I would pick him up at college in Philadelphia and head to King of Prussia Mall, a very large mall about twenty minutes away from downtown Philly. I had always been fond of Logan and valued his friendship with Tim, but since Tim's death, Logan and I had developed an even closer bond.

The three of us had a wonderful and happy time. We browsed in some extravagant stores and had a big laugh as one of the vendors in the middle of the mall continued to use his sales tactics to try and sell me more items. The mood was upbeat; we didn't grieve about Tim. Somehow, we just spontaneously had a lot of fun. We ate in the food court and I insisted on buying Logan a shirt since I had made some purchases for David. And then we headed back to the University of Philadelphia to drop off Logan. We didn't stay too long because I wanted to get home to spend a little time with Andy and Pete.

All right, now it was two down, one to go. Thanksgiving and Tim's birthday were over, and I just had to make it through Christmas.

Back in June, I had planned for the four us to go on a cruise for Christmas. We had never been on a cruise before, so we would not be able to compare it to when Tim was alive. More importantly, we would not be home for Christmas. Andy, Pete, and Dave agreed it would be a good idea, but Pete and Dave stated that they wanted to be home before New Year's Eve. Our excursion would begin on December 23 and we'd arrive back home on December 29. I decided we would exchange our gifts on the evening of December 22, since we were leaving early the next morning.

For the past couple of years, because I have way too many decorations for one Christmas tree, I had been decorating two: a live one with all the family ornaments on it and an artificial one with souvenir and nautical-themed ornaments. That year, I decided on only the artificial tree since we would be away. Another benefit to this plan was that I did not have to look at the important family ornaments with the special memories attached to them. Another small detail had been bothering me. On the gifts to our extended family I would always sign the gift tag "A, L, T, P, D" for Andy, Lisa, Tim, Pete, and David. I clearly decided I could never abbreviate "A, L, P, D"; instead I would write the names out.

We had a very nice time on the cruise. We all had dinners together, and Pete and David were off doing their own thing a lot of the time. However, we received some sad news on the night before we returned to New Jersey. On December 28, 2008, another local boy, Drew, who was Tim's age and had played sports with him, took his own life by hanging himself in his garage. When Pete called from the ship to talk to his girlfriend, she tried to hide her distress, but he knew something was very wrong. She then shared the tragic news with him, and he, in turn, shared it with us. I believe it was better that we found out while we were still away. It was hard enough to return home and realize, once again, that Tim was not there. I feel strongly that it would have been even harder to accept the news in our home upon our return.

With each young adult's death, I found myself reflecting on some existential questions. First I would wonder whether it is almost a little easier to be the mother of the first suicide victim. Maybe Tim was the "statistic," the one teenager in any given area who suffers such a tragedy. Each parent thereafter has to wonder if his or her child would have gone through with such an act if not shown by example. On the other hand, sometimes it's worse being the mother of the first one. I felt guilt wondering if Tim had caused all these deaths. Hearing that the deaths are not Tim's or my family's fault is somewhat comforting but does not eradicate the thoughts completely. Second, I would think even more about the things I may have done wrong. I thought maybe I was too strict and if I had been more lenient, Tim would still be alive. After one of the deaths I realized that those parents had been more relaxed than I about rules, so maybe my strictness was not the answer. I wondered if Tim would still be here if I had made religion a bigger part of our lives. Religion was very important to at least two of the other families, and one boy had been an extremely spiritual person himself, so maybe that was not the answer either. Also, that same boy had been involved with a girl who I thought was very mature and was a good influence on him. I wondered if Tim had been involved with an older, more mature girl if that would have helped. Of course, I wish with all my heart that all of these boys were still here, but in some way I learned through their deaths that there really is no definite answer to what I could have done differently.

# Chapter 38

After Tim's suicide threat and brief hospitalization in early January, every day was extremely stressful for me. I honestly don't think I ever let my guard down. I spoke to Andy and my sister Denise multiple times a day about each and every detail that was on my mind. Denise and I had the following discussion numerous times: If someone threatens suicide and doesn't go through with it, is it really a cry for help? Does that mean he really doesn't *want* to go through with it and wants to live? If the individual really meant to follow through, wouldn't he have just done so the first time so he could not be stopped? That is a common belief, but Denise had read somewhere that the people who threaten *are* the ones who eventually follow through. She worried daily that Tim would kill himself, but she knew I was doing everything I could and didn't have any new or different alternatives or actions to suggest.

Tim had been keeping a low profile, communicating as little as possible and unenthusiastically attending his therapy sessions. Accepting advice from Tim's therapist, we purchased and used a Breathalyzer to confirm that Tim was not drinking and driving.

One big change was that Andy no longer believed that Tim was "fine." He was now becoming more of my ally in the discussions with

Tim. I had previously thought that Andy's support would feel great, but unfortunately, it was only minimally comforting now. I needed to *know* that Tim would be OK, with or without Andy's support.

On January 20, our community suffered the loss of a sixteen-year-old, Bobby, who died in his sleep. At first a drug overdose was suspected because Bobby did have multiple illegal drugs in his system. Later information revealed, however, that he had died of complications caused by pneumonia and that the amount of drugs in his body would not have caused an overdose. Bobby was a neighbor who had attended the summer recreation program with my kids each year and had played Little League and school baseball with Tim and Pete. Tim took Bobby's death hard. He and Bobby had remained friends during high school. Tim barely ate for almost two days and moped around in his room even more than usual. Tim and Pete both attended Bobby's wake, but separately with their own friends. When Tim came home that night he frantically said, "I need five dollars." When I asked why, he became more agitated and just repeated himself. I gave him the five dollars; he went back out and then came home again about a half hour later, much calmer. When confronted the next day, Tim did not deny that the five dollars was used to purchase marijuana.

Right around this time one of Tim's teachers, Mr. Battaglia, contacted me for the first time ever, asking if things were going OK with Tim. I was so grateful for the call and realized it was probably time for me to reach out to Tim's other teachers too, both to provide information as well as ask for their feedback on Tim's behavior or any changes they observed in class. Mr. Battaglia had noticed that Tim was occasionally sleeping in class and was less enthusiastic and less interested in his performance, but none of the other teachers I contacted said they had noticed anything. I did speak to Tim about Mr. Battaglia's observation and also let him know that Mr. B. would be more than happy to talk to him at any time. While Tim did not deny the sleeping and lack of care, he clearly stated that he was *not* interested in talking.

At Tim's therapy sessions I would usually go in first, alone, because I wanted to make the counselor aware of what I considered important issues from the week. Next, Tim would go in alone, and then we would go in together at the end. Sometimes Andy would come too.

Occasionally Andy would go without me, only once or twice when I was too overwhelmed and angry to go. If I remember correctly, my refusals to go were frustrated responses to Tim's uncaring, unemotional attitude and his non-responsiveness to every conversation I tried to start.

At the session after Bobby's death, all of us heavy-heartedly discussed that Tim had now lost two friends to drug-related deaths. A friend from Wall, a nearby town, had overdosed on heroin the previous September. We pleaded with Tim to completely stop using alcohol, marijuana, and any other drugs. We continually tried to impress upon him that the substances were aiding him in masking the real issues, whatever they were, which I knew he did not want to try to uncover. Since learning of Tim's suicidal thoughts and depression, I had also done some reading, which revealed that marijuana could increase symptoms of depression by up to forty percent. This was one of the main reasons that Andy, the therapist, the psychiatrist, and I together were focusing on reducing the substance use. Tim said very little in response to what he considered our preaching. He had become quite proficient at letting us talk as much as we wanted and just tuning us out.

Until January, I had been worried about Tim's drug and alcohol use and his self-esteem. Now a suicide threat and another friend's death were added to the list. I thought about the possibility of staging an intervention, but knowing Tim, he would just run away. And his being eighteen years old would give me no power to try to force him back home. He really did not want help, yet I continued to spoon-feed him whatever help I could in small doses.

In the weeks immediately following Bobby's death, we noticed that Tim seemed to be going through his money very quickly. We suspected that he may have been taking painkillers again and began at-home drug testing regularly, rather than randomly as we had done previously. After one positive test result for opiates, subsequent results came back negative. Either Tim had chosen to stop because of the testing or because he was running out of money. Every other week, Andy and I were also seeing Tim's therapist without Tim to work on topics including trying to define what we could and could not accept in our house (pre- and post-graduation), what to do about disciplining our other sons, and how to stay calm. Tim's psychiatrist, who prescribed his meds, had added a mood stabilizer along with the antidepressant. She felt it would help with any bipolar aspects of his depression. Once again, we were agreeable to medication, now grasping at anything that would help Tim *choose* life. We also began going to a lab for a random monthly drug test, suggested by Tim's therapist and prescribed by our family doctor, to help ensure that he was not using any drugs other than pot. The blood tests were more thorough than the at-home drug test, and the results were consistent, showing only marijuana.

I was grateful for the tests showing *only* pot but prayed for a stoppage or at least a reduction in the pot smoking—something to allow Tim to face his problems rather than cover them up.

# Chapter 39

Sometime during the month of January I decided that I would plan a large celebration and fundraiser for the first anniversary of Tim's death. I thought this would keep me busy with all the planning and would give all of us—myself, my family, and Tim's friends—something positive to do as the date neared. I decided on the theme "Celebrate Life." My choice was highly motivated by David Cook's song "Time of My Life," the first song I felt I was able to enjoy during the early grieving. One of the posters I made and hung at the banquet hall contained the words to the song. The profits from the fundraiser would go to the Timothy Schenke Light of Hope Scholarship Fund.

Keeping busy seems to have been my best defense against depression. So in addition to planning the celebration, I took on several other projects simultaneously. We had the hardwood floors on our first floor refinished, which involved moving everything out, and while I was at it I cleaned out all the cabinets and storage areas. Each year a parent of a MHS senior lacrosse player hosts a fundraising dinner for the high school lacrosse team parents. I volunteered my home and coordinated all food contributions. At least fifty adults attended, and the evening was a hit.

While cleaning my room one day I came across a card I had purchased to give to one of my kids someday. The cover read, "To My Teenager... I Will Always Be There. Although we don't always see eye to eye I just wanted you to know that I will always be there for you when you need me..." The words brought tears to my eyes. I wished I could back up and give the card to Tim, whether he would actually have read it or not. See Appendix D to view all of the words on the greeting card.

I decided to write another letter to the editor of our local newspaper expressing my regrets about being unable to give the card to Tim, and sharing the content of the card. A few friends thanked me and told me that they shared it with their children. I never did end up giving the card to Pete or Dave. I still struggle with how much to express my feelings to them. I love them both dearly and would back up many years and be a lot *mushier* to each and every one of my three sons if given the opportunity.

I did a lot of the planning on my own for the Celebrate Life event, but I did involve some friends who really wanted to be a part of it and/or had special skills I could draw upon. My friend Sophie, a high school student who had led a large suicide prevention fundraiser the previous fall, and her mom, Andrea, helped a lot. A few months earlier, Sophie, who had never met Tim or me, wanted to initiate something proactive in our community after we had suffered three MHS student and alumni deaths, and she warmly invited me to join in with the planning and preparations. Truthfully, I think working with Sophie on that event helped give me the courage to begin my endeavor.

Friends helped with all kinds of detailed preparations for Celebrate Life, including soliciting and packaging gift auction items. My sister-in-law, Laura, helped design a magnet that I had mass-produced and sold at the event. I knew I wanted something with a peace sign and Laura offered me the choice of several excellent designs. I also decided that we would sell T-shirts in Tim's memory. Tim's friend Kevin came up with "Timfinite," which was just perfect for the front of the T-shirt. Kevin solely designed the artwork, and it was spectacular! He has a wall in his bedroom that he allows his friends to sign. He had traced Tim's signature, which said "Schenker," and had produced a color version for the back of the T-shirt. I ordered custom-made pens that allowed for four different messages to appear in a message window on the barrel. I kept the messages positive, keeping with the theme of Celebrate Life. Two local bands had volunteered to play and they, too, helped to make the event a tremendous success.

Of course, I had discussed the event with Andy, Pete, and David early on in the planning. Andy helped with whatever I asked, and Pete and David had some involvement. They approved of the designs for the magnet and T-shirt and helped sell tickets at the high school. Pete also secured one of the bands. I think they were both surprised and happy at how many of their friends supported us. At the event, Pete even took on a host role and did a great job working the crowd. David pretty much blended into the crowd. I believe the difference was somewhat due to their personalities and ages, but even more with the way they each coped with Tim's death.

The night of the event I definitely felt busier and more elated than I even remember feeling at my own wedding. I thoroughly enjoyed my wedding, but this was much larger, literally and figuratively. In addition, I was a lot more mature at almost forty-nine years old, and what could be more important than a tribute to my child? More than 350 people attended, and I genuinely had a wonderful time. I am so happy that I was able to take in all the love and positive emotion shared by so many of Tim's friends, our friends, and friends of friends.

In the weeks following, many people called me and sent notes letting me know how positive the atmosphere had been and how well they felt the evening went. The day after the event, April 26, the actual one-year anniversary date, we had a record warm and sunny day with ninety-degree temperatures. I believe I was still running on the positive energy; I rode my bike along the beach wearing a tank top and bike shorts, my favorite biking attire, which is most unusual for April in New Jersey. Shortly after that weekend I decided I would not turn the celebration into an annual event. I strongly believe something so perfect simply cannot be repeated. I would decide later whether I would publicly acknowledge the second anniversary of Tim's death, but if so, it would be in a different way.

# Chapter 40

*February 2008*

Several months earlier I had planned a family vacation to Hawaii during the upcoming school break in February. Tim originally did not want to go, but he knew he would have to, so he settled for a full tank of gas as his bribe. I believe that he must have wanted to go on some level or he wouldn't have settled so easily and the arguments would have lasted much longer. As the vacation neared, I was still feeling all the tension around what had occurred in January. As unnerving as it was, we had discussions with Tim to ensure he would not try to sneak any drugs onto the airplane. After we had finished packing, we ended up with a total of four suitcases that needed to be checked because Andy and I shared one larger bag. The airline allowed one free bag per person, and Tim noticed that I had suitcases registered to Andy, Lisa, Peter, and David, but not him. Tim called me out on it, claiming that I purposely had not put his name on a suitcase because I was worried about drugs. I lied and said I just went in alphabetical order, but I'm pretty sure he knew better.

While at the airport Tim asked if he could buy the book *Scar Tissue*, written by Anthony Kiedis, the lead singer of his favorite musical group, Red Hot Chili Peppers. I quickly said yes, happy to see him willing to read any book for recreation. During the flight Pete told me the book was Kiedis's autobiography and described his addictions and decision to stop using drugs. A glimmer of hope? Now I was *really* happy to have purchased the book! During the week, Tim became engrossed in the book, reading it at the hotel and bringing it in the car whenever possible. He explained that Kiedis's dog, which he'd now owned for four years, had never seen him high. I jumped on that one saying, "What kind of pet would you like? It can be all yours if you agree to stop drugs and alcohol." Tim thought I was kidding and said, "How about a snake?" I said, "I have to think about that one, but seriously, would you consider a pet?" Tim shrugged me off. I wish I had said yes right away to a snake, but in truth, I think he was just playing me.

The vacation turned out to be extremely pleasurable. Tim was more quiet than usual, and not his "boy always trying to be in the front," as he had been in his earlier years. I wasn't sure if that was due to actual depression or maybe the meds he was taking. In some ways he seemed to be more of an adult, spending more time with Andy and me instead of goofing around with Pete and Dave. We all enjoyed the sightseeing, the beach, the pools, the great hotel rooms, and most of all, our tour guide on the Duck Tour of Pearl Harbor. I truly wanted to kidnap my family and *never* come back. It was so fantastic. No arguing, no worrying (well, minimal worrying) about Tim harming himself, and no drinking or drug discussions. At Tim's next therapy appointment he admitted that he had a much better time than expected.

Tim had depleted his bank account just before we left for Hawaii. That winter I think Hoffman's Ice Cream had closed for a short period of time. Some years they stayed open all year, while other years they had brief closings during the winter. When I asked how he planned to pay for marijuana, he replied, "I guess I will have to stop." I gave "strict orders" to Andy and the grandparents that Tim was not to be handed *any* cash. If he needed gas, we would go with him and pay for the gas. If he pleaded for money for McDonald's, I would respond, "Get in the car, and I will take you."

Living this way was tearing me apart. My father had always handed the kids cash when he came over. Now, however, he stayed away, telling me that he just could not show up without handing Tim a twenty-dollar bill for gas. This upset me even more, but I had to adhere to my decision. I once gave Tim money to go to a movie with friends and asked him to bring the ticket stub back. Of course he didn't. Being the strong-willed individual that he was, I will never really know whether he stubbornly refused to bring the stub home or used the money otherwise. Around this time, I knew Tim was finding or earning money in different ways. Tim actually told me one method he had used to earn some money. One of his friends was failing English class, and Tim was writing his papers for cash payment. I also knew, through testing, that he had not stopped smoking pot, but perhaps it was less? I asked our doctor if there was a way to measure the amount of pot in Tim's system, versus just the yes/no test. But the doctor thought the yes/no testing was sufficient and that it wasn't necessary to quantify how much.

Tim also seemed a little less conscientious about his schoolwork and his behavior. I noticed fewer A's on some papers in his folders. Yes, Tim was enrolled in Advanced Placement U.S. History, Advanced Placement Calculus, and Honors Physics, but the A's had always come easily and he had prided himself on that. Tim was breaking curfew more often and received his first ticket ever for parking illegally near the school. He provided no explanation for these behaviors and agreed to begin paying us back for the parking ticket when he starting getting hours at Hoffman's again.

The Hawaii dream getaway was over. We were back to reality. Perhaps I should have seriously planned my "kidnap the family" idea and found a way to implement it.

# Chapter 41

Although I know better, I have at times wondered if the highs are worth it because the lows inevitably follow. The months of May and June, immediately following the successful Celebrate Life event, were probably the rainiest two months on record.

Around the third week of May, I made a decision that I think turned out to be a good one. In the past I had gone for an occasional body wrap. That rainy May, I found a business about thirty-five minutes away that offered an unlimited month of body wraps, "for one low price." Andy, being the supportive husband that he usually is, said, "Go ahead." I am happy to say that Andy and I don't argue much at all about financial decisions. We save our extravagances for important things, and for the most part we seem to agree on our priorities. Since Tim died, we probably have been freer with spending money than we were before. Oh well, a little less in the nest egg, but we're not struggling. Also, I would like to add that I am anything but a pampered woman. I've never had a manicure or a pedicure and I never plan to. I also don't wear much makeup, but confess I do color my hair. I tried to get the body wraps three times a week, but wouldn't miss anything important for them, like Pete's lacrosse games. While I did not lose weight, as they claimed, I relaxed. And this was a good feeling.

I had also toyed with the idea of seeing a psychic for a while and eventually scheduled an appointment for May 27, which happened to be another gloomy day. The visit was fairly positive, but I don't know if the psychic told me anything that truly could not have been discovered by searching the web. I was looking for something from Tim that no one could possibly know. Some of the information was general, some was just kind of weird, and some could have been obtained by reading the obituary, newspaper articles, blogs, or my letters to the editor.

While Tim did not speak to me directly during the session, my deceased father-in-law supposedly came through telling me that "he had the boy," and that I should stop beating myself up because Tim's death wasn't my fault. The psychic added that Tim was extremely hurt by my father-in-law's unexpected death in 2005 and wanted to be close to him. I explained that Tim always enjoyed being around Grandpa John; both grandfathers were his favorites. Grandpa John was playful and fun, and I feel he helped instill great values such as honesty, fairness, and respect in our kids.

The psychic also said I was a good mom and that I had raised Tim the way he needed to be raised. She feels that when a spirit is born, he chooses the parents he needs and Tim chose me, a loving and structured mom. She also stated that everyone's death date is predetermined on the day that they are born. She explained that Tim had contracted with God for a short life. Immediately after I left the visit I stopped for lunch and wrote down every little detail I could remember. I'm glad I did because some of the conversation was reassuring.

One warm June day, I was sitting on the beach alone and once again thinking about the "give it to God" dilemma from the night before Tim died. My thoughts were along the lines of, "Was I ready to accept Tim's death that night he did not come home? What if I actually gave Tim permission to take his life?" Shortly after Tim's death I recall Justine, Tim's ex-girlfriend, telling me that if it weren't for the unrelenting love and determination provided by Andy and me, he might have taken his life sooner. A moment later, while still pondering my thoughts on the beach, I felt Tim say "thank you" to me. Was it a voice? Even today I'm unsure, but it was very real. I also felt that my dog Ory was somehow present. When I got home a short while later, I sat on the couch, and Ory seemed more affectionate than ever. I honestly felt that Tim was communicating through Ory at that moment.

Similar to my feeling Tim's blankie rub my face the day of my first tattoo, seeing color in the sky the previous summer, and hearing my favorite song at two critical moments, I felt a real connection. These contacts are few and far between and I choose to believe they are real. This one was a little scarier than the others because of the message. Was Tim thanking me for arriving at the place to "give it to God"? I still do not know the answer, but what I realize, which is most important, is that I accept the life God has chosen for me.

# Chapter 42

*Late February–Early March 2008*

When I asked Tim if he knew anything about why Andy and I were being called into the high school for a meeting in late February, he said he knew nothing about it. The high school secretary had called, requesting us to attend a meeting regarding Tim, but would not provide any details. I repeatedly asked why, but was not given any information, which was extremely frustrating. The meeting was scheduled for February 25 at 11:00 AM, and we had told Tim so he knew when we'd be at the school. The principal and the two vice principals opened the meeting by explaining that in the aftermath of Bobby's death, our teenage neighbor who died one month earlier, some students had become worried about other students and began reaching out to the staff. Tim was one of the ten to fifteen students named as being perhaps troubled or involved with drugs.

I then opened the floodgates, both verbally and emotionally. It was ironic that these administrators thought they'd be telling *us* something about Tim. Boy, did they get an earful! I explained everything that had occurred—all the facts and all the feelings. After our discussion, they suggested bringing Tim into the meeting so he could see how much we all cared about him. Since Tim had been aware of our appointment and

I suppose he wanted to hide, he had gotten a pass to the restroom and had been roaming the halls for a while. Finally, when he was located, he entered the room with his sweatshirt hood drawn low over his eyes. After one of the vice principals gave her talk about the number of caring people in the room, Tim responded, "I'm not doing anything wrong in this school. I don't bring drugs here. I don't sell drugs here or anywhere else." I suppose he had his defenses already prepared. I was crying and said, "We love you and want you to live," but he withheld all emotion. Andy was basically quiet throughout the meeting, but I could see the tension in his face and his body. At home later, Tim had little to add except, "Mom, you were freaking out in front of all of them."

Yes, I definitely had been freaking out. I reminded myself that writing, for therapeutic reasons rather than for actual distribution, was an effective way of dealing with stress. Therefore, I wrote two documents: an advertisement and a letter to the editor of our local newspaper. The ad stated that if Tim died, I would not have a viewing or receive visitors because his death would have been such a waste of a life. It also said that I would not want to celebrate his life or give any type of recognition to his death. On February 28, 2008, I sent an email to my sister and my sister-in-law, which included the "fake" letter to the editor. I asked them to send it to the local paper if I were to die from a nervous breakdown or any other cause. The "fake" letter read as follows:

## OPEN APPEAL TO LOCAL ADMINISTRATORS, LAW ENFORCEMENT, AND PARENTS OF TEENAGERS

Dear Editor,

I am writing this letter to request three wishes. My first wish is for a full-time police officer to be placed in Manasquan High School. I know this is being addressed by those in authority. I also know that one individual could not be in all places at the same time. However, maybe it could prevent some of the drug use and other pranks, like the bomb scare last week. My second wish is for local law enforcement to avoid granting "breaks" to some of the local teens and their families. Although it may seem like a "break" at the time, it may not be in the long run.

Lastly, I would like more parents of teenagers to stop "looking the other way." Maybe if more parents opened their eyes, we could at least make a dent into peer pressure.

After much thought, I conclude that my primary reason for writing this letter is to prevent myself, and maybe some of you, from having to write an obituary instead.

—Lisa Schenke
Spring Lake Heights

I believe this letter in a way evolved into the May 8, 2008, letter that I did send to the *Coast Star*. However, the message and the tone ended up quite different. See Appendix A for the actual letter. At the time I wrote the "fake" letter I deeply feared that Tim might die, but I don't know if I actually believed it would happen. What an amazing difference between how I *perceived* I would feel and how I actually felt when Tim died. I had so much anger during those stressful months leading up to Tim's death that I suppose turned into sadness when my loss became a reality.

# Chapter 43

The previous summer, two of my friends, Nancy and Pat, gave me a pendant that contained a picture of Tim. I tried wearing it as a necklace and as a bracelet and eventually found a solution that was perfect for me. I bought a small crucifix on a chain and then added the pendant to the same chain. I positioned the two pieces so that the crucifix fell in front of the picture of Tim. I happily wore the necklace for about a year before I lost it. To date, I have never found it. At first I thought I wanted to replace the exact crucifix and pendant, but I could not find the same crucifix, not even in the store where I had purchased it the first time. Eventually I gave up on finding an exact replacement and decided to just wait until the right thing came along. I did look on the internet frequently, trying to help the right replacement combination come along.

Pete was now getting close to going away to college. We were experiencing the usual precollege conflicts: Pete wanted to come home at all hours, wanted to spend every moment with friends, and gave me more curt responses than ever, leaving both of us feeling nervous and edgy. We dropped Pete off at the University of Delaware on August 29, 2009. I kept my composure, but all the while I was very conscious that we had never reached this point with Tim. I felt that I should have two children in college now. Pete at University of Delaware and Tim at Drexel University in Pennsylvania. I imagine I will have these feelings when Pete or David gets engaged, gets married, has a child. Before Pete left, I told him that I would probably need to have contact once per day and to date, we usually do. I tried not to text Pete too often, but he was very good about responding and now he sometimes texts before I do. Happily, our relationship has improved with some space between us.

The only major issue Pete was facing was that he had to share a double room with two other roommates instead of one. The school explained that most "triples" would be resolved before the end of the first semester. Not only was the room overcrowded, but there was no air conditioning, and the month of September was proving to be a warm one. Lucky for Pete someone on his floor left and a few boys who were in triples within his building had the opportunity to state their cases as to why they should be the person to take the vacancy. The boy who was now without a roommate was also allowed to state his preference, and he chose Pete.

One Friday night in September, Andy, David, and I were out shopping. Just as I found the perfect replacement pendant for my necklace, a small oval with the inscription "Peace Lies Within" on the back, Pete called me to share some good news. Andy answered my cell phone and Pete said, "Can I talk to Mom?" I don't know what thrilled me more: the fact that I had found a pendant, the fact that Peter was no longer in a triple, or the fact that Pete wanted to tell me first. Well, maybe it's no contest after all.

# Chapter 44

*Early March 2008*

There were days that winter when I felt that David was my only motivation for getting up in the morning. I was always worried about Tim, and Pete had put up a protective shell that could not be penetrated. He appeared to be completely self-absorbed, only concerned with his own wants and needs, as if nothing around us had any effect on him. I can relate to this withdrawal. When I was an older teen, my family was experiencing a lot of emotional issues and I can remember being short with them and just fending for myself.

David, on the other hand, sometimes retreated to acting childish, which grated on our patience. But he still wanted to be with us and I suppose he was looking for some reassurance that he was *safe* and life was *normal*. Sadly, I can remember saying to David, "Please don't leave me or do anything to hurt me now. You are the most pleasurable thing in my life and my reason for getting up in the morning." My statement did not mean that I did not love Andy, Tim, and Pete; just that David was the only one with whom I was not engaged in daily conflict. In retrospect, I think it was a terrible thing to say. What extreme pressure to place on my young teenage child. I wish I could go back and erase that statement.

We gave David a drum set for his fourteenth birthday, March 7. I remember Tim saying, "I could never get a drum set. I thought he had to take lessons first to make sure he was serious about it. That's what you told me when I wanted a drum set." I was honest with Tim. I shared my feelings that, based on everything going on in our home, I probably had given in a little easier. David had been through a lot these past months. It broke my heart to say that, but it was the truth. I suggested that Tim take lessons with David or on his own, but he refused. I then proposed that David could share what he learned with Tim after the lesson, but he still said no. This is one of the conversations I revisit from time to time. It still causes me grief, and it's one of the incidents I refer to as my "recurring stabs."

# Chapter 45

*October 2009*

I t had been almost ten months since someone we knew had died by
suicide. The last of the local young adult suicides had taken place on
December 28, 2008.

One day I met up with an old friend, and we got into a conversation
about psychics. He highly recommended someone in northern New Jersey,
and I told him I would keep that person in mind should I ever decide to
visit a medium again. My first psychic visit had been five months earlier.
I guess the temptation became too strong, and I caved in on October 21.
Unlike my previous experience, this psychic told me some scary things.
Similar to my previous visit, I did not feel that I received anything from
the session to solidly confirm that Tim was communicating with me.
This psychic asked me to bring a blank CD because she routinely records
the session so that the client can listen to it again later. Once again my
father-in-law supposedly communicated with me, and once again I did
not hear from Tim directly. She felt that an evil force had been involved in
the previous young adult suicides and that the suicides would continue.

The next day I tried to listen to the CD of our session and discovered it
was blank. With Andy's help I tried to play the CD in multiple computers,
portable players, and our cars. None of them would play the CD. I called

the psychic on Thursday, October 22, to inform her and she said, "Very infrequently my recorder doesn't capture the session. Sometimes the spirit does these things." I was now quite glad that I did *not* have the recording and even more thankful that I had not received any assurance that Tim was definitely communicating with me because I had been told that the contagion of suicides would continue… and it did.

On Friday morning, October 23, Andy called me to let me know that the tracks in Sea Girt, a neighboring town, were closed and that maybe something had happened again. I finished with two clients and picked up David from school about 10:15 AM, as previously planned, because I had to take him for preoperative bloodwork for an upcoming tonsillectomy. There seemed to be way too many people and a strong police presence at the school. When David got into the car, he told me that Matt, currently a senior and also from Spring Lake Heights, had died. No one, however, knew any details of how or why. I told David about Andy's earlier message that the tracks in Sea Girt were closed and said that hopefully it was just a bad coincidence.

After driving only a few short blocks my phone started ringing, and David began receiving text messages. Sadly, Matt had stepped in front of a train in Sea Girt earlier that morning. I was a nervous wreck and probably glad that David was with me when we found out. Pete had been away at college for almost two months, so I quickly decided to call because I wanted him to find out the news from me before hearing it through the grapevine. Pete was supposed to have taken a calculus quiz that afternoon, but he chose not to go. Matt was the closest to Pete in age, and he had played recreational and school sports with Tim, Pete, and David. He had also played traveling soccer with Pete and had been coached by Andy.

Throughout the day, friends checked in on me in person, by phone, and through texts and emails. It was an emotionally draining day, not only because of dealing with another death, but also because of my worrying about Pete, who was almost two hours away at college. It was a Friday, and Pete did choose to come home for the weekend, so Andy went to pick him up. Pete went back to school Sunday night, then came home again the following Wednesday for the funeral. The exact cause of Matt's suicide may never be known, but his family strongly believes that his use of a particular acne medication is what led to his tragic decision to take his own life.

I had stopped by Matt's family's home that afternoon, but I was told that Cathy, Matt's mom, was not up to seeing any visitors. That night Cathy's sister called me and asked if I could stop by and speak to them. I was exhausted and somewhat fearful, but I knew right away that I would go. Several times during the previous eighteen months since Tim's death, I have tried to be supportive and act as a positive role model to people grieving over the loss of others or suffering themselves. I feel good about reaching out to people I know or people who knew Tim. I remember trying to reinforce to Cathy and Matt's dad, Pete, that with time, they would be able to resume their lives. I continued to stress how important their choosing life was for the sake of their daughter, and I explained that my other two sons had been my primary motivation for getting through each hour in those early days of grieving.

I think I drew strength from a conversation I had with Vicky, the mother of Drew who had taken his own life the previous December while we were on the cruise. Weeks after Drew's death, Vicky told me that a specific memory she had of me had helped her get through her son's funeral. She remembered seeing me in the supermarket, sometime after Tim's death, engaged in conversation and laughing. She had not interrupted me at the time, but she said she had always remembered how content and adjusted I seemed. I was very happy and honored that the memory had helped Vicky through that tough day and hopefully many days to come.

The morning of Matt's death, David and I talked in the car on the way to and from his bloodwork appointment. I remember saying to David, "If I was a parent of a boy from our area, I would be so worried right now. Not that our family is excluded just because one child has died." The best part of my day was when David responded, "God would never do that. How can you even think that? You are the one who believes in God." I happily assured David that he was correct. On the way back to the school, David and I decided that he would return to school, even though some students were getting released to their parents. We agreed it would be better to spend time with his friends and supportive teachers than to sit at home doing nothing. I suggested that David stop in to see the student assistance counselor, and he said he would. David had also hurt his foot in a soccer game the day before, so he had planned on seeing Mr. Hyland, the athletic trainer, as well.

I was somewhat panicked because on my recent visit to the psychic, only *two* days prior, she had stated that the suicides would continue. It took me a while, and several visits to David C., to calm down. After all, there was a 50-50 chance that the psychic would be correct about the suicides continuing. Also, how do I know that the messages coming through to this medium were from God or Tim? The messages could be coming from the dark side as well as the light. I eventually committed to David C. that I would never visit a psychic or medium again. I have been tempted, and even made and cancelled an appointment once, but I stuck to my word.

# Chapter 46

Tim began to get hours at Hoffman's Ice Cream again by mid-March and that meant money in his pocket. A drug test, performed by me around March 25, showed he was positive for opiate painkillers. I immediately called Tim's psychiatrist because I thought she would react most critically to the drug use, and she got us in for an appointment on March 27. Even though the appointment was during the business day, I asked Andy to come too, and he willingly agreed. During the session, Tim committed to *not* taking a painkiller again. We seriously discussed that he would have to voluntarily go for in-patient treatment or choose not to live in our house if he tested positive again. Taking illegal drugs is dangerous enough, but now that Tim was on prescription medication and he had previously had suicidal thoughts, we would not tolerate the painkillers at all. We decided that we would drug test again in a few days because the previous pill, or pills, taken approximately March 25, might still show a positive result if we tested today.

On Sunday, March 30, Andy and I decided to perform another drug test. We both entered Tim's room and he adamantly refused to take the urine test, stating that he wanted one more day. I remember Tim saying things like, "I hate you. You lied to me. You said you would do the test on

Monday. I'm going to kill you." Based on Tim's lack of cooperation, Andy started looking around the room. He opened Tim's top desk drawer and found a thick wad of tissue. When he unraveled it all, it revealed a bullet. This was a complete shock. We had suspected Andy might find drugs, but a bullet? When questioned, Tim replied, "I got it from a friend and just decided to keep it." Andy was furious, and I was worried sick. Andy yelled, "Where did you get this? What are you planning to do with it?" Tim said, "Nothing, I just wanted to keep it." I was crying and yelling, "We love you! We want you to live! We want you to be happy!" Tim had been lying in his bed. I remember that I lay on top of him, hugging him, trying to let the feelings penetrate him. But there was no response from Tim: no hugs, no words, no emotions.

To this day we have never found a gun, but God only knows why he had the bullet. We insisted on the drug test, and it showed positive again for opiates, which caused us to believe he snuck in at least one dose after the psychiatrist appointment. We had also heard a bunch of change clanking in Tim's pocket. When he emptied his pocket, it was a large quantity of quarters. He said he found a roll of quarters outside of the local convenience store and had emptied them into his pocket. At the time I had no idea where the quarters came from. But about a month or so after Tim's death, I realized that my state quarter collection was missing from where it was stored. I don't know for sure, but I believe the quarters in Tim's pocket on March 30 must have been my state quarters. Where else would they have gone? Thinking about those quarters is another "recurring stab" for me.

Tim went to school the next morning. I worked my morning hours and then started making phone calls to decide what we would do regarding the positive test result and the bullet. I remember calling Jerry, our police officer neighbor. Coincidentally, Jerry suffered a seizure later that same day, and his wife joked that my conversation with him had set things in motion. Both the therapist I had been seeing at the time and Tim's therapist recommended that we take action at this point. One of the two suggested that we involve the county mental health services because the bullet could indicate that Tim planned harm to himself or others. Another serious concern was that Tim had uttered, "I'm going to kill you."

After dinner that night, Tim was upstairs playing *Rock Band*. I had previously arranged with Monmouth County Services that I would alert them as to when he was at home. Two individuals entered our home along with the D.A.R.E. officer, Officer Gunnell who knew Tim, and persuaded him to go with them for evaluation. This time Tim's exit from our house was calm, unlike the scene on January 3 when he had to be handcuffed to be removed. Once admitted, this time Tim knew the ropes and knew his rights as an adult. He refused to sign the forms that would allow the county hospital doctors to speak with his outpatient doctors. He also refused to allow Andy and me to talk to the hospital doctors.

Tim told us that he had agreed to go to the substance rehabilitation unit of the mental health facility he had been admitted to back in January. That same night, we arrived at the mental health facility before the ambulance that was transporting Tim. When I spoke to the front desk staff, they informed me that Tim was being admitted to the adolescent mental health unit, once again, not the rehab. Being the nervous wreck that I was at that time, I argued that they must have it wrong.

When Tim arrived a short while later, he smirked and told us that he did not agree to rehab. He had agreed to go to the same unit he was in last time because he knew he could talk his way out of there easily. We felt there was too much of an artificial distinction between the definitions of the units and the line between child and adult. Because Tim was eighteen years old, he was considered an adult who could make his own decisions. However, because he was still a high school student, he was placed in the adolescent mental health unit. The result for his father and me was the ultimate level of frustration, and the feeling of helplessness that stemmed from it.

At this point it seemed that Tim could not push us away fast enough or hard enough. A few years down the road, I read *History of a Suicide: my sister's unfinished life* by Jill Bialosky. Jill's younger sister, Kim, had died by suicide. A quote from Kim's journal that appears in Jill's book states, "My plan now is turn mean. Blow-off my friends and family and make everyone hate me. If nobody cared then it would be easy to leave. I'm so trapped." When I read these lines, I was immediately taken back to the episode with Tim at the mental health facility.

I pleaded with the caseworker to keep Tim hospitalized. The caseworker on this visit was a different woman from the last time, and I thought she was a knowledgeable, persuasive person. At the family meeting prior to Tim's release, I did think that she played every card she had, but could not penetrate Tim's outer shell. Prior to that family meeting, the caseworker told me that only two topics seemed to bring a sparkle to Tim's eyes. The first was Drexel University, and the second was his brother David. We jointly planned to hone in on these topics. With tears in my eyes and a lump in my throat, I told Tim that David had recently stated, "Why doesn't Tim come to my games or drive me around like Aidan's brothers do?" Tim's eyes did open wider and he asked, "Did David say that?" I said something like, "Yes, Tim, he wants you to be a part of his life, please consider how much he loves you." Tim looked terribly sad but barely responded.

Although Tim was no longer in a relationship with Justine, they continued their friendship and had lengthy phone conversations late into the night, often three to five hours at a time. Tim dated a few other girls, but he seemed to remain focused on Justine. I later learned that he had written her a long note during this second hospital stay but I have never learned the contents.

Against our better judgment, Tim came home again on April 4. However, he seemed to be a little happier and less oppositional. Throughout the next few weeks, the at-home drug tests read negative for any type of painkiller and positive for marijuana only. On April 20, known as National Weed Day, Tim told us that he was going to quit smoking pot until graduation. Andy had been trying to bribe Tim with fixing his car, while I had continued to nag Tim about the importance of keeping a clean record so he would not lose the Drexel University academic scholarship. Whether it was the bribe, the threat, or both, this time he took the offer. I was somewhat skeptical and said, "The test results will tell." Coincidentally, the addiction specialist appointment we had been waiting for was scheduled for April 21. Tim, Andy, and I attended the appointment, which lasted at least two and a half hours. I remember the doctor saying, "If you do not modify the course you are on, there is a fifty percent chance that you will be dead before age twenty-five. If you live, you will die young, maybe fifties or sixties, and will barely or minimally achieve any of your goals."

The doctor next asked Tim, "What percentage of you wants to get better?" Tim responded with an answer of twenty percent. This was another knife to my gut. Although that percentage was terribly low, I tried to focus on the positive by reinforcing to myself that at least it was not zero. Tim was prescribed a drug that is known to reduce cravings. Supposedly the drug had been proven effective for alcohol and some drugs, but there was no proof for marijuana. Tim was not thrilled with going to the appointment or starting more meds, but knew he had no choice if he wanted to continue to live in our home and have us pay for college.

The pharmacy did not have the drug in stock, so it had to be ordered. The doctor had instructed us to start with a little sliver the first day, and then increase by one sliver of a pill at a time. Tim had his first dose on Thursday, April 24. He appeared to be stressed about the number of pills he was taking per day, which seemed worse than it actually was because some of the dosages caused him to take more than one pill per day of the same med. He had commented to us and to a few friends that he was taking seven pills per day, which was true because of the dosages plus an antibiotic he was taking for a sinus infection and a sleeping pill he had requested during his in-patient stay. Considering how little emotion Tim had been exhibiting, was this a big issue for him? Was he perhaps feeling doomed? Beyond help?

Conversely, Tim seemed to relax and enjoy himself a little more throughout the remainder of the week. A few nights, Tim had invited David to his room to watch TV, and he joined Pete and David in our hot tub, which he had not done for a long time. Tim had shared with his AP Calculus class that he felt he was a shoo-in for a score of four on the upcoming exam scheduled for early May. AP test grades range from one to five, with a score of three and above considered a passing grade. I found out later that he had contacted some of his old eighth-grade Heights friends asking to shoot hoops, but none of them were available. That Thursday night, April 24, my parents were visiting and he socialized. He had also gone out with Andy to pick up Italian ice for everyone. While I didn't quite relax or let my guard down, it did feel great to see Tim interacting more and possibly even enjoying being part of the family again. It seemed like we had reached a small respite.

# Chapter 47

When David returned to school the day of Matt's death, he went directly to Mr. Hyland because the student assistance counselor's office was overflowing with students. After they spent two hours together, Mr. Hyland called me sounding very optimistic and saying that he and David were going to spearhead something positive for MHS. When some of the previous suicide victims had died, David hadn't liked the clothing that had been designed in their memory. I remember that he disliked a line from a Red Hot Chili Pepper's song that read, "And in the end, my friend, we will all be together again." David felt that the words on the clothing should be uplifting and promoting happiness and life, rather than talking about death.

David and Mr. Hyland had a meaningful conversation and decided to get together again early the next week to formulate a plan. Mr. Hyland had a great idea to contact the Life is good Company to ask if MHS could use the slogan and if they would donate. Within two weeks, Mr. Hyland and Dave had organized a Life is Good Day to be held at MHS on December 11. Based on donations from the Life is good Company and other fundraising efforts, a major surprise was planned. Also, with the support of the administration, an essay contest about why life is good was held. David and some other grieving students and friends were among the judges. What an amazing coincidence that David had hurt his foot and sought out Mr. Hyland that day! Maybe it was no coincidence at all, but rather a divine intervention.

Two days before the event, which happened to be Tim's twentieth birthday, David spoke about the plans for Life is Good Day at a teachers' staff meeting. Mr. Hyland called me afterward to let me know how well David had spoken and shared that there was barely a dry eye in the house. Several teachers also contacted me to compliment David. These positive feelings definitely helped me get through Tim's birthday. On the evening before the event, Andy and I helped set up, along with a few other families who had suffered tremendous losses. The staff at MHS consists of so many wonderful, caring people.

Life is Good Day, December 11, 2009, was a tremendous success. The afternoon consisted of music by a rock band made up of high school students, talks by motivational speakers, essay awards, and a proclamation from the mayor of Manasquan that Life is Good Day would become an annual celebration. Then came the big surprise: Life is good T-shirts *for every student in the school!* I was amazingly proud of David, Mr. Hyland, and the numerous other students and staff members involved. The following year, Dave became cofounder and president of the newly formed Life is Good Club at MHS. The club now has more than one hundred members and continues to offer fun, positive, and motivational activities. I am extremely happy to report that since the birth of Life is Good at MHS, we have not lost another current student or recent graduate to suicide.

The theme "life is good" pretty much carried into my personal life that winter too. I do not like the cold, and I usually find January through April to be the slowest time of the year. Last winter I had busied myself with projects and planning the Celebrate Life event. Now, in February 2010, I somehow miraculously convinced Andy to look at condominiums in Florida. I have always had the dream of moving to Florida. However, I realized that we wouldn't be moving anytime soon, so why not have a vacation place. At this point in time, the housing market was doing so poorly, especially in Florida, that my dream seemed doable. Before approaching Andy with the idea, I had worked out the details of how we could take a line of credit against our current house at a reasonable interest rate. After some thorough research and planning, we ventured on a three-day trip and came back with a signed contract!

Pete, David, and many of our other family members and friends could not believe that Andy agreed, but the deal was honestly too good to pass up. Happily, January and February had been filled with research and planning, and now March and April were filled with bargain shopping. While I am not a clotheshorse, I absolutely love home decorating. We planned to rent a truck and drive to the condo in July after David would be out of school and done with soccer tournaments. Being who I am, I planned every detail for the condo: some new furniture, some used furniture from our house, including Tim's bedroom set, every window curtain, dish towel, and more. In some way, I feel the condo is a gift from Tim. If we had been trying to finance three college tuitions, I would have never considered the purchase. Since we would have somehow managed three sets of tuitions, why not take on a different form of debt in place of the one that no longer exists. Looking back now, the condo was a great purchase, providing us a regular getaway and, more importantly, a way to spend time with Pete and David as they grew older.

I was thrilled with the prospect of having more getaways and opportunities to spend time with my family, but I still yearned to have some type of concrete symbol of Tim closer to my heart. For a while I had been thinking of getting another tattoo, something on my inner arm, specifically dedicated to Tim, so that I could see it much more easily than the cross on my outer ankle. I was considering something with ocean waves and the sun because I love that setting and I feel close to Tim when I'm at the ocean. One day I saw a heart on Facebook that seemed to contain everything I wanted: ocean waves at the bottom, a sunrise in the middle, and a lightly decorated sky at the top. I loved it and decided to have Tim's name written inside the sun. One cold, rainy day in March I finalized my decision and got my third tattoo on my left inner forearm, just below my elbow. When asked, "Will this be your last tattoo?" my response is, "I don't know. That depends on what life throws my way."

# Chapter 48

Friday, April 25, 2008 was Tim's fifth day without smoking pot, based on his decision to stop from April 20 through graduation. All I could do at this point was encourage Tim's decision to stop and pray that he meant it. He went straight out with his good friend Johnny and a few other friends after school without stopping home at all.

When I checked in with Tim around dinnertime, he admitted that he had been physically fighting with some of his friends while at Johnny's house. He didn't sound happy, but said everything was OK and that he was not coming home for dinner. Through talking with Johnny after Tim's death, I learned that there was a second issue. Tim thought Justine had responded immediately to a text from Johnny while ignoring his texts, and that had upset Tim greatly.

I can surmise that the stress of being off pot for five days was getting to be too much for Tim, based on my own judgment and some Facebook posts I was able to dig up a few weeks later. At approximately 7:30 PM, Tim called me, admitting that he had smoked again, and told me that he did not feel good. I urged him to come home, but he refused and stayed out for the remainder of the evening. I tried to explain to him that maybe the marijuana had hit him stronger after having been away from it for a few days or that maybe the pot had been laced with something else. The "laced with something else" argument had been a common one from me. I had always emphasized that Tim did not know what he was actually buying. During the call, Tim briefly explained that he had had a rough afternoon, but now he was out with his friend Gary, whom he had not seen in several months because Gary had moved to south Jersey. He ended the call by saying that everything was now fine.

Throughout the evening, I had texted back and forth with Tim a few times, asking where he was, how he was, etc., like I always did. At this point in Tim's young adult life, his curfew on weekend nights was 1:00 AM. When he did not arrive home by 1:15, I began calling his cell phone. He finally answered at about 1:30 AM, and I asked, "Why aren't you home?" Tim responded, "I'm not coming home tonight." I next asked, "Are you asking to sleep out? Where are you going to be?" Tim replied, "I don't know, but I am not coming home."

Tim hung up the phone, and I texted a few more times, stating that he was not given permission to stay out. But Tim never replied. I finally called again, and this time Tim answered. I reminded him that if he did not show up, he would find the door locked in the morning and his cell phone disconnected. Again he didn't respond, but just hung up. I was now wide awake and crying. If I remember correctly, Andy, as might be expected, said, "Let's go to bed; there's nothing else we can do."

As mentioned earlier, I had been reading *Medjugorje*, a book about the Virgin Mary sightings that have occurred in Yugoslavia since the 1980s. I am a Christian, but I am not a practicing Catholic. After trying to leave the book under Tim's nose for a few days and his taking no interest as I had expected, I began to read *Medjugorje* myself. The book frequently said that we, as humans, cannot take control of everything. We must "give it to God." This was the night I repeated "give to God" as I lay awake in bed.

Thinking back, I have contemplated, "What is the 'it' in 'give it to God'?" What *was* I giving to God? I believe I was giving up control, which no longer belonged to me, or perhaps never did in the first place. I think I was accepting that Tim was an adult now and was free to make his own choices.

I woke up about 7:00 AM on Saturday morning and saw that Tim was not home and that he had not called, so I called our cell phone carrier and had his cell phone disconnected. Approximately a half hour later Tim called from Gary's house and asked, "Can I come home?"

I said, "Yes, if you are willing to accept the consequences."

"What are the consequences?" Tim asked.

I replied, "You'll find out when you get home."

"OK," was all Tim said.

"Do you want me to come pick you up?" I asked.

"No, I'll walk," Tim replied and then hung up the phone.

When Tim entered the house about twenty minutes later, I was relieved to see him but angry about his behavior of the previous night. He did not look or sound any different from his usual quiet and unexpressive self. I said, "You are not allowed to use the car, and you are grounded until your next therapy appointment on Wednesday. You have now pushed me past my final limit." Tim had no response whatsoever to my pronouncement. I next reached for a drug test and asked him to give me a urine sample in a bathroom cup. As I read the test results, I noticed a different positive result than I had ever seen before. The THC reading for marijuana was positive, as usual; the opiates reading, for painkillers, was negative; however, this time the reading for cocaine was positive. I was beside myself. I showed it to Tim, and he stated, "I did *not* do cocaine." I asked if he was lying, and he adamantly said, "No. I'm not lying." I then reverted back to my "laced with something" discussion and said, "Maybe the pot you had last night was laced with cocaine. Do you remember telling me that you didn't feel good after you smoked?" Tim once again said, "I did *not* do cocaine." I desperately wanted to believe him, and truthfully, I did.

Tim went upstairs to his room, and I started worrying that maybe he'd find the hidden car keys and try to run away while we were out during the day. He hadn't been grounded for quite a while, and I knew he wasn't going to take the punishment well. While Tim was upstairs, Andy woke up and came downstairs. When I asked him if he would take the battery out of Tim's car, he agreed to my request and headed outside. I don't honestly know what I was more afraid of at that moment: that Tim would take the car and run away or that he might try to kill himself by crashing the car. For some reason, I now vividly remembered that during our discussion back on January 3, the only day that Tim was honest with me about his suicidal feelings, he had told me that he was going to drive his car into the middle barrier of Route 70 in the town of Brick. Little did I know that one week earlier, Tim had come up with a new method of killing himself.

When Andy came back inside, he suggested that maybe we should turn Tim's phone back on. I argued against it, stating that we should stick to our word and reminding Andy that Tim had not come home last night. Months later, Andy finally told me that he has suffered over the phone disconnection. He sometimes wondered if that had caused Tim to take his life. I've tried to reinforce to myself and to others that one decision alone probably didn't cause Tim to take his life. This was the first and only time Andy shared this—for that matter, any—recurring painful thought.

Tim spent that entire day in his room. He had borrowed David's cell phone periodically during the day, and I later learned that he told Justine that he could never admit to us that he had used cocaine. Throughout Tim's high school years he had been unwaveringly against cocaine, not only in his expressions to us, but also to his friends. I would imagine that the decisions to *both* smoke marijuana again and now try cocaine were weighing heavily on Tim's mind.

# Chapter 49

*April 2010*

I used to love spring, but now I have mixed emotions. I realized this one Saturday morning in early April. As a primarily nondepressed person, I have learned through reading that for those who suffer from depression, spring can be the most challenging season. They can be made more depressed by the increased birth in nature and surge of life. As I was driving to a client's home one Saturday morning, I experienced that "high" from the warmth, brightness, and spring feeling in the air. But then, almost immediately I started crying, thinking about how Tim must have been suffering.

A few years ago I attended a speech given by Mike Reynolds, whose brother Bill died by suicide on Monday, May 5, many years ago. Mike is an inspirational speaker and has written a book, *Surviving Bill,* to help others, specifically sibling survivors of suicide. He explained that, statistically, May is the most common month, Monday is the most common day and, as in the case of Bill, the fifth is the most common day of the month for suicides. As April 26 approaches each year, and the Japanese cherry tree in front of my house erupts, I can feel that "pull" of darkness at this time, so I think I understand in a small way what those with serious depression are going through.

I had thought long and hard about whether to celebrate or how to celebrate the upcoming second anniversary of Tim's death. I had spoken to David C. and a few other close friends about an idea I had to combine the acknowledgement of the anniversary with some sort of anti-marijuana campaign. It never came to fruition, however. There just seemed to be so many obstacles with logistics and issues with peer pressure that I abandoned the concept.

On the morning of April 20 I happened to be on Facebook, and I noticed someone posting something about Weed Day. I don't know exactly how widespread this is, but April 20 is known by some as National Weed Day. I then posted on my page, "Today is Weed Day. If you dislike this day, please check 'like' on my post, and I will know that you mean 'dislike.'" I then left to go to my next client of the morning. When I stopped home between clients, I had at least eight 'likes' already. I focused on the name of one of Tim's friends, Vincent, whom Tim used to smoke pot with, but whom I had never spoken to. I wrote a quick, personal message to Vincent letting him know that he had made my day. When we chatted online that afternoon, Vincent admitted that he still smoked but clearly realized how much pot had curtailed his motivation and added to his depression. We shared a lot of feelings, and I can only hope that he finds, or has found, his niche and has a happy future.

Meanwhile, by then I had received several comments, and I was posting meaningful and heartfelt information on my page. By the end of the day, I believe I had thirty-five 'likes,' several of which were from teenagers. Throughout the next few days I realized that even though I had cancelled my idea for an anti-marijuana campaign, I had fulfilled my personal need that day on Facebook. Overall, Facebook has been so helpful to me during my grieving process. I often read people's posts on Tim's memorial page, and I have been fortunate enough to get to know so many more of Tim's friends via Facebook, either by chatting or meeting in person. I enjoy being able to express my feelings through my own personal posts. Additionally, many teens, young adults, and parents have reached out to ask me for help or tell me their story.

My family, friends, and those who follow my posts on Facebook and early letters to the editor in the local newspaper know how strongly I am against all illegal drugs, including marijuana. I believe marijuana is addictive and is a gateway drug that leads to use of other drugs. I am convinced that it was one of the largest contributors, if not *the* single largest contributing factor, in Tim's death. Yes, this is my opinion based upon my personal experience, and I have had so many discussions about it with Pete and Dave that they can probably quote me, word for word. I sincerely hope they never smoke pot, but, if they do, they had better *never* let me see, smell, or know about it in any way because I will *flip*!

After Tim's death, Andy and I got to know his friend Gary. He has grieved deeply and loves Tim as a brother. On numerous occasions, Gary has told me that he and Tim never did any drugs other than pot together. While I'm glad to hear that, I still cannot condone looking the other way regarding pot-smoking because of the excuse that it's "not a hard drug." OK, now I'll get off of my soapbox—I promise!

All that week and to this day, I continue to talk to Tim's friends. Sometimes I reach out, other times they do. Not too long ago, before Tim's twenty-second birthday, a friend of Tim's texted, "Hey Lisa. I just want to say that people and myself really find inspiration with all your positive posts and comments on Facebook…And know that we are all thinking about you this holiday season and especially tomorrow…Keep being strong and we love you…Now back to studying for my finals. I know Tim will help me out…"

The actual two-year anniversary date, April 26, 2010, passed uneventfully but with one special memory. Sometimes at night, David comes into our bed in his sleep. He is barely aware of it, if at all. When he unconsciously slips in, he stays on the outside in his own space. David doesn't seem to be looking for body contact the way Tim did when he used to ask me to lie in his bed when he couldn't sleep. On the night of April 26, David not only came into our bed, but draped an arm and leg over me, exactly the way Tim used to. I woke up and did not move or go back to sleep, just wanting to enjoy every moment of this. Whether it was Tim's communicating to me through David, or David's needing me in a different way that night, it was wonderful. I happily added this incident to the short list of times I have felt a direct connection to Tim. I felt great for days, and I believe this experience helped get me through my fiftieth birthday, five days later.

# Chapter 50

We sat down for dinner that Saturday night, April 26, 2008, just Andy, Tim, and me. The day had been long, but productive. I had needed to stay busy as a way to prevent myself from worrying about the previous night. Andy and I attended Pete's high school lacrosse game, shopped for mulch and a few plants, and test-drove a possible new car for me. When asked to sit down to dinner, David said he wasn't hungry because he and his friends had eaten pizza an hour or two earlier. Peter was at a friend's house, which left only the three of us at the table. Our rectangular kitchen table seats six. Andy and Tim's seats are at the two ends, David's and my seats are on the outside, with David next to Tim and me next to Andy, while Pete's seat is on the inside, his chair backing up to a large window, next to Tim and across from David. However, tonight Tim was down at his end by himself, since Pete and David did not join us. Blank-faced and very quiet, not unusual behavior for an eighteen-year-old who is grounded, Tim began eating our steak dinner. Steak happens to be his favorite, cooked medium-rare, and I hoped he would eat well that night to help balance out his system.

Breaking the silence I asked, "Did you call Theresa, or stop by Hoffman's?"

Tim replied, "No."

I next suggested, "Why don't you go see her in person, talk to her face-to-face? I think it will help if she sees you in person."

"Yeah, maybe," Tim said, but unenthusiastically.

Theresa, the manager at Hoffman's, had promised to put him back on the schedule two weeks earlier, but he still hadn't been given any hours. I added, "You should get a haircut before going because we know she'll say that you need a haircut with your hair this length." Tim kind of nodded and maybe grunted a "yeah." After finishing the steak and refusing to eat his potato and salad, he went back to his room. Andy and I put the leftovers away and decided to take a quick ride to a department store that was having a closeout sale. Andy then left the kitchen and headed upstairs.

Moments later Tim walked down the stairs and informed me that he was going to the nearby local convenience store. Today's punishment, a severe combination of penalties because of what had transpired the night before, had stripped Tim of his car and his cell phone.

"You know you're grounded," I responded.

"I'm going anyway and I might not be back," Tim said flatly.

I considered this threat a bluff. But at this point what choice did I have? Tim could leave if he chose to go.

"Then don't," I said in utter frustration. Or at least that's what I think I said. My exact words still remain a blur to me.

# Part IV

# Chapter 51

*In the aftermath of Tim's death*

The night of Tim's death I was not allowed to talk to Tim's friend Johnny, or any of his other friends who had any contact with him that night because the police needed to interview them first. The outcome of the interviews created no conflicts or questions. It was officially determined that Tim had acted completely voluntarily. However, through conversations with Johnny, Justine, Logan, Gary, and others during the next few days, I was able to piece together a little more about the events of April 25. According to Johnny, Tim had been very angry that day with a guy who had expressed interest in Justine. The fight, between Tim and his own friends, which Tim had described to me over the phone, supposedly had been a fight to prevent Tim from trying to go after the guy. After getting together with Gary, Tim went to a sweet sixteen party at a local home, where he met up with Johnny and the friends he had fought with earlier as well as numerous other friends. Johnny has indicated that everyone was getting along fine, while Gary believes there was still some conflict.

Logan, who was planning to attend Philadelphia University, only fifteen or twenty minutes away from Drexel University, later told me that he and Tim had a long, happy conversation at the party. He said Tim had seemed very excited, stating how happy he was that they would be at nearby colleges. They would get together on weekends, and Tim would help Logan with schoolwork when needed.

After Tim's death, Logan grieved over this conversation, feeling that Tim had betrayed him. Logan and David have shared the feeling of betrayal. David also felt betrayed because Tim had seemed to get closer to him during that last week. Of course, I don't exactly know why Tim acted as he did, but I have shared with Logan and David that I believe Tim was completely conflicted. One side of him wanted happiness, relationships, college, etc., but the other half was afraid, fearful of the future, and terrified of continuing to live because of the way he was feeling. In *History of a Suicide: my sister's unfinished life*, Jill Bialosky discusses psychologist Erik Erikson's concept of "embryonic darkness." Referring to her sister Kim, Jill states:

> The teenage years into the early twenties are a period during which we discover who we are going to be. Filled with self-doubt, Kim was caught between her family's expectations of her and her own feelings of diminishment. Sometimes dropping out of high school or college, flirting with drugs and sex, may lead a young person to find her own voice. She may be in the middle of a crisis and must go to the other side before finding out what matters to her. Those who weather the storm sometimes emerge as people of talent and creativity. The birth of creativity can come from the risk of intense self-annihilation. And the sensitive, at times self-destructive, tentative person is perhaps someone who lives at the balance of these two conflicting forces. Sometimes I saw one side of Kim—a flash of the girl with the knowing smile—and then it would vanish. And then I'd see another side—anxious, serious, a dull look, like a dirty penny in her eyes.

When reading this material a few years after Tim's death, I immediately thought back to my conversations with Logan and David.

By spending time on Facebook shortly after Tim's death, trying to locate posts Tim had written on friends' pages, I did substantiate my speculation that Tim was experiencing more difficulty avoiding pot than he had anticipated. I read one specific posting that said, "Yes, it's only been a few days and harder than I thought it would be." I believe another stressor for Tim was that he and Johnny had committed to stop smoking pot together. When Tim could no longer hold out on April 25, Johnny told Tim that he was sticking to the plan.

I was later told that Tim did four lines of cocaine that Friday night, but I have no idea whether it was in the early evening or in the early hours of the morning. I was also informed that four lines was a large amount for a first experience. I believe the "coming down" from the cocaine partially contributed to his irreversible decision, but to what extent, I will never know. Another area of concern has been whether the anti-craving drug, recently prescribed, had any negative impact on Tim. Because he had only three very small doses of the medication, I don't think it could have had much effect. Honestly, I don't even know if the antidepressant and the mood stabilizer were helpful or harmful. Whenever I asked Tim if he felt any side effects, he would reply, "I am fine." I strongly dislike the word "fine." When someone asks me how I am, I might say, "Great, good, so-so, miserable…" but I will *never* say, "Fine."

When Tim had told Justine that he could never admit to Andy and me that he had used cocaine, I believe he was extremely sad that he had disappointed us yet again. Even worse, I think he felt that he was *totally* losing control. Tim had always been a stubborn, decisive individual. He liked things black and white, and I suspect he was suffocating in the gray. But gray is reality. How I wish Tim had possessed the coping skills to navigate through gray.

Just before leaving the house that night, Tim had phoned a few friends from David's cell phone just to say, "See you later," or, "Let me know what you are up to tonight." When Tim called Gary's house, Gary was not there to answer the phone. Because of this, Gary has agonized about not having been available to Tim that night. I have tried to comfort him by expressing that Tim may have been calling him just to say, "See you later," as an unofficial good-bye, the same as I suppose he had done with his other friends.

Sometime after dinner on April 26, Tim called Justine and asked her to meet him. Justine had been the only person in whom Tim had honestly and consistently confided his suicidal feelings throughout the previous months. Approximately one week earlier, Tim had told her that he had come up with a surefire method for ending his life: jumping in front of a train. Going back to January, Justine had pressured Peter to tell us that Tim was suicidal and that she knew about our later insistence on the doctor visits and medications. She claimed that she had not known Tim had been telling us that everything was "fine." She has said she had been unaware that we, his family, did not know that the suicidal thoughts had continued.

When I later asked, "Why did you agree to meet him at the tracks that night?" she told me that she was unable to persuade him to meet her elsewhere. Justine also told me that while they were at the tracks, Tim had said that I didn't even care about him anymore. I suppose that his statement was based on my defeatist response, "Then don't." I know in my heart that Tim knew this was *not* the truth. I believe he had to tell himself that in order to go through with his plan. Our last words to each other are the worst of what I referred to earlier as my "recurring stabs."

Because Tim had discussed suicide with her on other occasions, Justine did not consider April 26 to be different from any other day. She has also shared that she did not believe Tim would go through with taking his life. I can only guess that he wanted Justine to be the last person he spent time with. As Tim ran away from Justine, toward the tracks, he tossed his favorite camouflage sweatshirt to her. I imagine that was his parting gift.

Do I wish the two of them had never met at the railroad tracks that night? Do I wish Justine had told someone that Tim had come up with the idea of killing himself by jumping in front of a train one week earlier? Of course I do, but I wonder if the final result would have been any different. Might it have it been a different night? A different scene? If significantly later in time, a different girl? As the Serenity Prayer teaches us, I have learned to accept the things I cannot change.

# Chapter 52

*Second anniversary cycle*

Throughout June and into July 2010, I was packing and organizing the items we planned to take to our newly acquired Florida condo. On Saturday, July 8, we picked up the rental truck and loaded it all afternoon in the heat, humidity, and intermittent rain. A few of Pete's and David's friends helped out. After our work for the day was done, I went out to pick up some pizza. Just as I started my car "Someone Saved My Life Tonight" began playing on the radio. I felt chills and knew that Tim approved of our starting a new chapter of our lives enjoying our condo in Florida. This was now the third time that Tim reached out to me through my favorite song. Just recently, I brought one of Tim's "blankies" to the condo and realized that it was the final touch to make me completely comfortable there.

The story now takes me to the end of what I consider the second "anniversary cycle," August 9, 2010. I view the period between Tim's death on April 26 and the depositing of his ashes into the ocean on July 31 and then into the cemetery on August 9 as the "anniversary cycle" because the earthly distribution and burial did bring some sense of closure to Tim's death. I had been jotting down notes and considering the idea of a book for the previous few months, and finally, on August 9, 2010, I found the courage to begin writing my story.

Within the first ten days after Tim's death, I had lost seven pounds due to stress and eating very little. Then within the next year and a half I gained back those seven pounds, plus an additional seven pounds. I believe that was due to my overcompensating, not only in the area of food, but also in child rearing. I feel that I became less strict than ever about what I was eating, and I had been walking on eggshells all too often with my other two children. While I had never backed down from confronting my own issues, I had become too fearful of conflict with Pete and David. I was not happy at this end of the spectrum and knew I had to find my inner balance. As I progressed through the initial phases of writing this book, I returned to my normal weight and seemed to find myself in a more comfortable and confident place.

Not long ago, I had a dream that Tim and Pete were going away together with other friends for their spring break. In the dream, Tim was a student at Drexel University, and Peter was a student at University of Delaware. After thinking about this dream for days, I brought it up at my session with David C. I had often dreamed of Tim alive and well, at age eighteen and under. I have also dreamed that Tim is dead, when I dream of current times. This was the first time I had ever had a vision of Tim alive at a stage in life that he had not yet reached. David C. helped me to recognize that maybe the dream was a sign that Tim and Pete would have become friends later, which might be believable if I consider that they'd no longer be living together. I so regret that they did not have the opportunity to become friends, as my sister, previously my archrival, and I did in our adult lives.

I recently pondered the fact that Tim would now be over twenty-one years old—what *I* consider an adult, unlike the government which considers eighteen-year-olds adult enough to go to war and to make their own medical decisions. After watching so many of Tim's and Pete's friends mature, I yearn for an adult relationship with Tim. At the time I started writing this book, I hadn't yet had these thoughts. Yes, I had grieved the fact that I wouldn't see him graduate college, get married, or have children, but I don't think I had yet visualized a mature relationship between us. Most likely this will become another of my "recurring stabs" that I will learn to quiet—not to eliminate but to put into its proper place.

I'm happy that we gave Tim the chance to hike in the Grand Canyon, snorkel in Hawaii, see the sun set over Cadillac Mountain, take a Pink Jeep Tour in Sedona, meet Mickey and Minnie Mouse numerous times, take in the beauty of Bryce Canyon, stand where Orville and Wilbur Wright flew the first airplane, deer-watch in the Poconos, climb lighthouses, and experience so many other diverse, wonderful things. I think we showed him how to enjoy life; unfortunately, he couldn't draw upon so many great memories in his time of despair.

I am both proud and grateful for how well Andy, Pete, and Dave are doing. I am extremely proud of Pete's adjustment and success in college and of his college entrance essay, which reflected on his relationship with Tim and on the steps he's taken in his recovery. And I'm proud of David's overall positive outlook and energy and his leadership in the Life is Good initiative at MHS. A large percentage of the time I am capable of feeling happiness, and for that I am proud of myself. I think I will always have an ongoing sadness too, and I don't want that to ever go away. I think it's about learning to live with the sadness rather than trying to find ways to eliminate it. I used to cry over happy endings to movies because I was happy. Now I cry over happy endings because I realize Tim will not have them. Sometimes a good cry is just what I need. I feel life's pendulum, which swings between accomplishments, tragedies, emergencies, never-ending distractions, and everything else we face each day. Like the pendulum, the aim of life is equilibrium. I continue to strive to find my inner balance.

I love and miss my son, and I have spent endless hours asking myself what I could have done differently. If at all possible, I would have tried to project the positives at *all* times throughout his childhood. I don't know how possible that goal is. As parents, we all reach our limits and shout, respond negatively, and sometimes even curse as we raise our children. If I could have, I would have tried to be more conscious of always creating a positive environment. I have unceasingly thought about whether I would be stricter or more tolerant. I think about so many parents who seriously don't know and don't even try to know what their kids are up to.

The bottom line for me is that I am, and always have been, an involved parent.

I do not know if I did all I could have done, but I do know that my eyes were wide open and that love drove every choice I made.

# Updates from the Author–2013

Since completing *Without Tim*, there have been a few changes in my life. I'll start small: I rode on a train. Not from Spring Lake or one of the local train stations, but from a station about twenty-five minutes north, in Long Branch, New Jersey. I rode to New York City with my friend Dianne in September 2012. In bigger news: we moved to Point Pleasant, New Jersey, approximately fifteen minutes away from Spring Lake Heights. The move was a bit of a downsize and a way to distance myself a little from my immediate surroundings. However, it is close enough to maintain our jobs, friends, and coastal New Jersey lifestyle. I had been thinking about it for the past few years, but patiently waited until David was no longer in high school.

David is a happy, active young adult, commuting to Monmouth University. Dave did get his first tattoo, which reads, "*The* Pursuit of Happines*S*" with a blue *T* and a gold *S* for Tim's initials. Peter, a recent graduate of the University of Delaware, sorely misses college life, but will be moving on to his next phase of life by attending Seton Hall Law School. Part of Pete's motivation for pursuing a career in law was the tragedy involving his friend Andrew.

Andy enjoys his job and house projects and has returned to one of his earlier hobbies, boating, often with David. Andy and I are still doing well as a couple, enjoying our Florida condo, bicycle riding, and enjoying the Jersey Shore to the fullest. Please visit my web site, www.withouttim. com, for updates about my family, as well as to find inspirational material, resources, and other news.

Regarding the suicide contagion in southern Monmouth County, I wish I could say that we have not lost any more teens or young adults to suicide since my manuscript left off in the summer of 2010, but sadly, we have. The excellent counseling and support continue, though, and I am relieved to state that the tragedies are less frequent and we are on the mend.

Tim's friend Gary's struggles with addiction and depression became worse before they became better. However, I am happy to share that as of this printing Gary has been "clean," to use his words, for almost a year and a half. I mention this here not only because I am proud of Gary, but also because Gary and I hope it offers encouragement to others.

I am eternally grateful to have made so many wonderful friends since Tim's death, both locally and through my web site. I continue to connect with struggling teens and young adults, as well as with parents who are grieving. I do this on a small scale, primarily under the radar, which is the way I like it. Readers can get in touch with me via the web at www.withouttim.com. I try to be honest and approachable, and to provide help where I can.

Sincerely,

Lisa

# Appendix A
# Letter to the Editor

To all who are suffering from the tragic loss of Tim Schenke,

Although this may be impossible, I am trying to offer some insight into Tim's difficulties. Because he was such a closed person with Andy and me, please know that my interpretations may be somewhat inaccurate. However, I do feel I know my son in ways that no one else did and I have feared this outcome for the past few months.

I first want to explain that Tim was not an "addict" physically. He came to rely too heavily on marijuana for self-medication purposes. I guess he was suffering so strongly that he became emotionally dependent. The use of other drugs became a larger issue after the death of Bobby Bannick, and even then, there was no "dependency". Tim did try to follow our house rules and accepted our punishments, sometimes without major complaints. I wish the last few months could have been happier and lighter; without so much time spent arguing, drug testing, going to different doctors, trying anti-depressants, mood stabilizers,... The problems were building for much longer than a few months—it's just that the last few months were so much more serious. I am so thankful that our family had such a wonderful, argument-free time in Hawaii during February. I wished we never had to come home.

I want to say to the kids: please do not turn to alcohol or drugs to deal with your problems/insecurities. There are so many people who want to help you. Andy and I personally offer to help you. To the parents: please do not accept that "it is only pot" and pot is not addictive. Yes, there are plenty of kids who drink and smoke on the weekends and maybe that is just "typical" teenage behavior. However, there are so many other kids who are not just "having a great time", they are in tremendous pain. Tim always felt that he did not have many friends, and that after being friends with someone for a while he perceived that he became annoying. He knew he was easily bored, overactive, and intense, but I guess he could not internally accept all of his positive attributes and how much he gave to others and was loved. To all parents, educators and law enforcement: please try not to "look the other way". Tim used to plead with me to leave him alone; to act like other parents who just didn't want to know. That was probably the theme of our most common argument. In some ways, I wish I was less demanding and just showed simple love, unconditionally. But, in other ways, I think he wanted/needed my harsh hand and that it contributed to the great person he was.

Lastly, I want to share a little background information for anyone reading this who did not know/know of Tim. He was a scholar, athlete, volunteer, and tutor, not only through school, but to so many friends informally. He was planning to attend Drexel University, College of Engineering and had received a significant merit scholarship. Unfortunately, throughout Tim's life, his self-esteem did not match his capabilities and I believe that was part of the problem. There are, and will continue to be, so many unanswered questions.

My love to all,
Lisa Schenke
Spring Lake Heights

# Appendix B
# Athlete of the Week

# Schenke wins game against Raritan

It's a moment that every athlete wants the chance to have. An opportunity to be the hero.

For Manasquan junior midfielder Tim Schenke, he had that chance last Thursday in a game against Raritan.

As the game went into its second overtime tied 1-1, it looked as if a tie was inevitable.

Tim got a pass from junior Andy Pinnella right around the top of the 18-yard line.

Tim fired a low left-footed shot that grazed the goalie's fingertips before finding the back of the net.

"I was so pumped up. It was a big division game," Tim said. "I really thought it was going to end in a tie, so I was excited to win it."

The win helped Manasquan continue its solid play in A Central.

"It's great to have a bunch of kids who can step up and make a play," Squan Coach Mark Levy said. "I was real happy for Timmy."

"I just ran towards the sidelines and everyone mobbed me," Tim said. "I normally don't get to score big goals like this."

Tim is an honors student at Manasquan.

He's interested in several colleges, such as Delaware, Maryland and Virginia.

> *"I just ran towards the sidelines and everyone mobbed me. I normally don't get to score big goals like this."*
>
> — **Tim Schenke on the celebration after scoring the game-winner in double overtime against Raritan.**

Tim hopes to become an engineer and his favorite subjects are math and history.

Tim's parents are Lisa and Andrew and he has two younger brothers, Peter and David who are 15 and 11, respectively.

Tim graduated second in his class in eighth grade and is currently ranked fourth in his class.

In his spare time, Tim likes to watch professional soccer and also play street hockey.

"As a soccer player and just make sure I hustle up and down the field," Tim said. "As a midfielder I'm just trying to create opportunities for my teammates."

TIM SCHENKE

# Appendix C
# Tim's First College Essay

The most influential person in my life is my mother. Since the day she gave birth to me, she has influenced me to do well in everything I do, and I love her for it. Without her encouraging me to do my best, I wonder if I would be in this position, writing an essay to get into college.

Since day one of my life, my mom has been setting high standards for me. She has helped me achieve many goals by providing support, options, and sound reasoning. I thank her for setting these high standards because it genuinely helps me work toward my full potential. So far in my life, I view myself as intelligent and successful. Even when my mom doesn't speak the words, I know she wants me to study for tests, do my best in sports, and try my best. My mom has always stressed my ability to earn A's in all of my classes, and I have become so accustomed to it, that I now expect A's from myself. I truly love my mother for helping me set goals and achieve them.

Secondly, my mom's life greatly impacts me. From the time that she was eight years old until she was seventeen years old, my mom's father was not living in the same house as the rest of the family. This was probably very difficult for her because those were crucial years in her childhood and adolescence. Without my father, I imagine I would be less motivated and comfortable with my life than I am right now. My mom had to deal with her own life as well as help take care of her younger sister. Although her family was not financially secure at that time, she still managed to attend Montclair State University and graduate with honors. I feel that she has been triumphant in life, having two different careers and raising a family. Shortly after age 40, my mom planned and successfully executed a career change from systems manager at a large corporation to personal fitness trainer.

In conclusion, the greatest influence in my life has been my mother. She has always expected me to do my best and has set high goals for me. My mom's past, as well as her current life, encourages me to do well. I look forward to successfully completing college and continuing to set and achieve meaningful goals.

# Appendix D
# To My Teenager... I Will Always Be There

Although we don't always see eye to eye
I just wanted you to know
that I will always be there for you when you need me...
No matter what life brings,
You will always be my child
who I love beyond measure
No amount of rebellion
could turn my face away from you
or stop my heart from loving you
I want you to have all the best life can offer
and you are so deserving of the best
My greatest wish has always been for your happiness
So as you go through these years
—and I know they are hard
because I've been a teenager too
remember two things:
First, know your own worth.
You are a beautiful person outside and in.
And second, know how much you are worth to me.
You are more precious than anything.
—Joanna Lucy Laird

# Resources

## Hotlines

American Foundation for Suicide Prevention (AFSP): 800-273-TALK (8255) A National Suicide Prevention Lifeline www.afsp.org

2nd Floor Youth Helpline: 888-222-2228  A confidential and anonymous helpline for New Jersey's youth and young adults ages 10-24. Call for everyday AND serious problems www.2ndfloor.org

www.suicide.com/suicidecrisiscenter/whycall.html can help individuals understand why to call and what to expect if you've never called a suicide hotline. National hotline and state-by-state hotline numbers are also provided.

## Grief / Suicide / Loss of Child

American Foundation for Suicide Prevention (AFSP) www.afsp.org

Compassionate Friends—Grief support after the death of a child www.compassionatefriends.org/home.aspx

Suicide... read this first www.metanoia.org/suicide

Recovery Books—The Recovery and Self-help Bookstore www.recoverybooks.com

Suicide Awareness Voices of Education www.save.org

American Association of Suicidology, Suicide Loss Survivors www.suicidology.org

## For Teens and Young Adults

To Write Love on Her Arms (TWLOHA) is dedicated to presenting and finding help for people struggling with depression, addiction, self-injury and suicide www.twloha.com

Understand your self-worth and help promote it in others www.youcannotbereplaced.com

Personal stories of hope, survival, and overcoming obstacles so that you can know that you are not alone www.yourenotfinished.com

If you are thinking about suicide, you are a suicide attempt survivor, or you are a suicide loss survivor, check this out. American Association of Suicidology www.suicidology.org

Caring About What's Beneath the Skin: Online Resources for building Self-Esteem www.dailyglow.com/pages/skin/self-esteem-resources.html

Teen Line—For teens who have a problem or just want to talk to another teen who understands www.teenlineonline.org

Useful tips and valuable links to help you feel better about your body www.admedia.com/media-and-body-image.php

**For Parents**

Child Behavior Help—Young children through adult children, includes child-rearing, respect, anxiety, depression and more www.empoweringparents.com

Parents, The Anti-Drug—Drug information, parenting advice, and more www.theantidrug.com

Parents section of www.youcannotbereplaced.com

For Mothers: www.withouttim.com/why_do_women_cry.html

**Lisa's Book Picks for Suicide and Grief Recovery**

*No Time to Say Goodbye: Surviving the Suicide of a Loved One* by Carla Fine www.carlafine.com/works.htm

*History of a Suicide: my sister's unfinished life* by Jill Bialosky www.jillbialosky.com

*Surviving Bill* by Mike Reynolds www.survivingbill.com/index.htm

*The Lessons They Taught Me* by Paul Battaglia www.lulu.com/shop/paul-battaglia/the-lessons-they-taught-me/paperback/product-5627831.html

Note: Paul's book is a wonderful story of Tim's Advanced Placement Calculus class "family" 2007-2008

SEE www.withouttim.com for details on:

AFSP Out of Darkness Walks

You're Designed to Shine: a program to inspire young women to identify their dreams, have faith, and develop the tools to achieve their goals

# About the Author

Lisa Schenke was a longtime systems analyst turned personal fitness trainer, but with her son Tim's suicide in 2008, she took on another line of work. She became passionate about getting the message out to struggling teens and young adults to *celebrate and embrace life*, and assisting others through the grieving process after a loss of a child or loved one. Lisa began by reaching out to her own community, and then realized she had a larger voice.

Lisa is an entrepreneur at heart who works for herself and loves to organize and promote uplifting activities. In the summer of 2012 she implemented You're Designed to Shine, a program to inspire young women to identify their dreams, have faith, and develop the tools to achieve their goals. Lisa was very active in fundraising and promoting the first annual Jersey Shore American Foundation for Suicide Prevention Out of the Darkness Walk in 2011, where she spoke as a suicide survivor. This walk was awarded the Most Outstanding First Year Walk by the AFSP at the national level. Lisa was involved in the Hold On suicide prevention fundraising efforts in 2009 and 2010 to benefit 2NDFLOOR Youth Helpline, a statewide New Jersey program. In 2012 she spoke at a University of Medicine and Dentistry of New Jersey suicide postvention training program to teach counselors how to work with family members in the immediate aftermath of a suicide. She's been featured everywhere from the *Star-Ledger*, New Jersey's leading newspaper, to MSNBC.com, to the American Association of Suicidology newsletter.

A New Jersey native, Lisa currently resides in Point Pleasant, about two miles from the ocean, with her husband and two younger sons. Readers can contact her via the web at www.withouttim.com.